THE BACKSMART FITNESS PLAN

A TOTAL-BODY WORKOUT TO STRENGTHEN AND HEAL YOUR BACK

ADAM WEISS, D.C.

McGraw-Hill

New York Chicago San Francisco Lisbon London Madrid Mexico City Milan New Delhi San Juan Seoul Singapore Sydney Toronto

Library of Congress Cataloging-in-Publication Data

Weiss, Adam, D.C.
The backsmart fitness plan : a total-body workout to strengthen and heal your back / by Adam Weiss.
p. cm.
ISBN 0-07-144338-X
1. Backache—Exercise therapy. 2. Backache—Prevention. 3. Physical fitness. I. Title.

RD768.W4275 2005
613.7'1881—dc22 2004022728

5 6 7 8 9 0 FGR/FGR 0 9 8 7

ISBN 0-07-144338-X

Interior photos by Wesley Park

This book is for educational purposes. It is not intended as a substitute for individual fitness, health, and medical advice. Please consult a qualified health care professional for individual health and medical advice. Neither McGraw-Hill nor the author shall have any responsibility for any adverse effects arising directly or indirectly as a result of information provided in this book.

McGraw-Hill books are available at special quantity discounts to use as premiums and sales promotions, or for use in corporate training programs. For more information, please write to the Director of Special Sales, Professional Publishing, McGraw-Hill, Two Penn Plaza, New York, NY 10121-2298. Or contact your local bookstore.

This book is printed on acid-free paper.

CONTENTS

ACKNOWLEDGMENTS

This book never would have seen the light of day if it weren't for the support and commitment of others. They include, first and foremost, my family:

My mother, who has always shared a passion for books and life with me.

My father, who taught me what a promise really meant and his commonsense approach and better solutions toward obstacles in life; he is always there when I need him most.

My wife, for her wit and sense of humor that always makes me laugh. My best friend—always dream big because there is no one who's going to take it away from you!

My children: Brandon, you always bring joy and happiness to me, allowing my inner child to play games with you and remind me what life's really about. Rachel, the sunshine of my life, your warm and generous ways truly warm my heart every day.

Peaches, Tiger, Sleepy, 24-Karat, Diablo, Honey: thanks for the best companionship and joy a boy could possibly ever have. We will meet again and feel the wind in our hair and feel the thunderous pounding of our feet hitting the ground as we run at full speed!

Thanks to my staff, who had to make my chicken scratch look readable from odds and ends of recycled papers each day they came into the office.

To my copyeditors, Bette, Kat, and Ellen, who taught me the economics of the English language.

To my agent, Andy Zack, for his determination, guidance, and support for this project.

To my editor, Natasha Graf at McGraw-Hill, for her support and foresight.

To the models, Kimber, Kristin, and Stephanie; and Wesley, my photographer.

And finally, to my patients, for trusting me and my methods of care with each challenge you brought my way.

The people and their stories in this book are real; just their names have been changed.

INTRODUCTION

Even in that moment, I knew I had done something that would affect my life forever. It was my freshman year in high school, in the weight room. I was lying on my back, bench-pressing 245 pounds, at a body weight of 145 pounds. Later in life, I would think back about that moment and imagine how differently things might have turned out if I had not been as strong as I was.

It was wintertime, and I was exercising in a cold weight room, which I now know is not good for the joints of people at any age. But this was the early '80s, and football coaches taught exercise classes. A sign on the wall in the weight room read "NO Pain, NO Gain!" I remember the weights moving up and down, increasing by 10 to 20 pounds each set. On my final set, I began to struggle while pushing up the weight. Instead of helping me by grabbing the bar, my friends encouraged me to keep trying. Up to that point, my form had been good—feet flat on the floor, arms shoulder-width apart.

Then it happened. I arched my back a little higher, and a loud pop could be heard throughout the room. The bar had almost fallen on me due to the sheer pain running through my body. I thought a lightning bolt had hit my spine and raced through my legs down to my feet. I began to sweat profusely and slowly sat up. I thought that if I could walk, I would be OK. But in the back of my mind, I realized something terrible had happened to my back.

Over the years, I went to many specialists, from a neurosurgeon to an occupational therapist, looking for a way to overcome the constant pain. I eventually started repeating the strenuous exercise routine I was able to do before the injury, but I failed and frequently reinjured myself. Throughout my college years, my body became deconditioned, and I began to gain weight, which I had been unable to do before my injury no matter how much food I ate. I realized things were different now; I needed to work out to keep the weight off and at the same time *not* hurt myself.

I went back to martial arts and conditioning exercises, and I was able to build stronger and more flexible muscles by combining toning and stretching exercises. I ultimately became competitive again. I have shared this method of exercising with others of all fitness levels, and they have also achieved their fitness goals (eliminating pain, losing weight, and improving health); years later, I call this the BackSmart Method.

WHY THIS BOOK?

There seem to be many so-called experts out there offering advice and telling people that one exercise is better than another. But who is to say which is more effective—Pilates, free weights, exercise machines, yoga, or one of the many other choices—for spinal pain? Many of us still have numerous unanswered questions about exercise and back pain.

As founder and director of a premier sports medicine center for athletes, I am uniquely qualified to write this book. I have treated thousands of patients—from stay-at-home moms to professional athletes—and have helped them turn their lives around, from being overweight, depressed, and in pain to enjoying a more joyful lifestyle by eliminating their pain and allowing them to get into the best shape of their lives. I have been able to instill in them the understanding that an essential connection exists between exercise and health, thus helping them recognize that the benefits of regular exercise go well beyond the cosmetic. Exercise is the single most important factor when it comes to preventing back and neck pain and heart disease, lowering cholesterol, decreasing cancer risk, losing weight, increasing energy, and reducing stress.

The BackSmart Fitness Plan will become a vital tool for your health and that of your family. It is a book to which you can refer time and time again. It will help you recognize certain risk factors for spinal problems (from sprains and strains to the more severe herniated disk injuries), which, if diagnosed early and treated appropriately, can be prevented. Additionally, it offers you a variety of programs and exercises to follow that will help you lose weight and get into the shape you've always wanted—an athletic look.

I had been thinking about writing this book for more than 20 of my 37 years, many of which were spent dealing with back pain and using cross-training to overcome the problems and excel at any sport I chose, while getting into the best shape I could be in. So, I decided it was finally time to share this unique form of exercising for a full-balance workout. I believe I can make a difference and help people get into shape, regardless of their age or their past attempts at starting an exercise routine.

WHAT YOU'LL GET FROM THE BACKSMART PROGRAM

Getting into shape is not as difficult as some people make it out to be. Our bodies have a muscle memory that thrives on being healthy and strong; all that is needed is to eliminate the mental barriers that sabotage the process of getting into shape.

This book is for women and men of all ages who want to improve their health and increase their longevity. The information provided is based on my personal experience with back pain. By following my instructions and suggestions, you will be able to create an exercise program that will give you a healthier and stronger body. This book has separate sections, allowing you to build a foundation of good exercise habits and then move on to explore different movements for your desired results. These results can include fat loss, increased flexibility, reduction or elimination of pain, and improved strength and endurance within six weeks of starting the program. Most exercises can be performed with a minimum of equipment and can even be done at home.

The program starts with a routine of stretches and calisthenics (without using weights) that will develop muscles. It then moves into more advanced routines (working the abdominal muscles, using weight machines, and using free weights) to sculpt and define the body further. The exercises in all sections are interchangeable, making the book an even more versatile tool for working with individual differences. You'll learn how to set physical goals and how to monitor and evaluate your progress using the calendar and workout journal. No matter what your age, you will be able to benefit from this program.

HOW TO USE THIS BOOK

Each person who reads *The BackSmart Fitness Plan* will use it differently. However, I hope everyone will read the chapters in Part 1, which detail how the program is organized to provide you with the tools you need to obtain the shape you want.

There is a natural learning curve for most of us, whether it is for mastering new computer software or for successfully cooking a new recipe, and each of us has a unique way of reaching that goal. In Chapter 2, I share my own struggles with pain and my long and difficult return to optimum health and fitness. Because of fatigue and the wear and tear on my joints and muscles, I could no longer exercise as I had before—running, lifting weights, and performing martial arts all in the same day. I needed to train smarter—to exercise in a way that would not break down muscle tissue. I decided to exercise more frequently rather than do it all in one intense workout, since I knew that a smaller amount of stress to joints and muscles would require less recovery time. Because I experienced less pain and soreness between workouts, I was able to exercise more often and ultimately improved my fitness level. I have applied the lessons of this personal experience to my patients with successful results, regardless of their age or gender. Taking the quiz first in Chapter 1 will allow you to identify familiar patterns and become aware of potential downfalls in your exercise routine. Scoring your results will help you identify telltale signs that indicate that your workouts are not effective. These poor patterns of exercising could lead to an injury or, if ignored, could lead to more serious problems such as disk herniation, lower-leg or hip pain, and chronic tendinitis in your joints.

I have included in Chapter 4 certain flexibility exercises (referred to as the BackSmart Daily Dozen) that I have used personally for more than 20 years and have taught to patients and at athletic seminars for the past 11 years as well. Just performing these exercises daily will increase your flexibility and help prevent back pain. You will feel more youthful, more relaxed, and less stressed as you incorporate these exercises into your daily routine. This improvement alone should be an eye-opener to your potential.

Chapter 5 focuses on core training of abdominal muscles, which are important not only in their vital function but also for the support they give to the rest of the torso. The torturous workouts I have witnessed over the years in and out of the gym would lead most people to forgo any attempt to develop a well-shaped midsection; some of these exercises have even caused neck pain. This chapter will take away the mystery of how to obtain a well-defined, shapelier midriff, to serve as a more supportive stabilizer for the spine, by exploring the many angles and combinations of exercises needed to achieve results.

The Swiss ball and balance drills make Chapter 6 one of the more fun and challenging chapters for most people, as incorporating balance into your workout will not only enhance your sensory output but also improve your coordination and speed, thus helping to prevent injury to the spine. The desired result is an athletic look and not a bulky bodybuilding appearance. You will improve your posture and add a step of confidence to your stride.

Chapters 7 and 8 will show you a few new twists to the same old exercises done in gyms and homes around the world. Why is it that one person can do only bench presses and have perfectly shaped chest muscles, while another person can do three to five different exercises for the chest with little progress to show for the efforts? Don't chalk it all up to genetics! There are more ways to stimulate muscle fibers than you thought possible. Information in these chapters will give you the arsenal you need to achieve the ultimate shape you desire without compromising the spine in the process.

The chapters in Part 3 will show you how to combine these new exercises into a highly charged and effective workout routine, giving you details on how to maintain that physical and mental edge needed to succeed in reaching your goals through diet and using a training log. I will conclude with discussing in detail commonly occurring injuries associated with exercising and how to prevent them.

Remember to follow the sequences of movements laid out in each chapter, and you are on your way to a healthier, leaner, stronger, more flexible, and pain-free athletic body.

A WORD OF CAUTION

It is imperative that you consult with your physician before you embark on this, or any, exercise program. Some of the exercises are strenuous and are not suitable for everyone. This book is not intended as advice or assurance to any specific reader regarding his or her ability to perform this program safely.

PART I

Starting Off Right

CHAPTER 1

TEST YOUR FITNESS IQ

Wouldn't it be nice if you could take some kind of quiz to see if you were susceptible to back injury or to determine if, say, push-ups were the right exercise for your build—or if you should stay away from push-ups because you may be prone to shoulder problems due to your body type? This chapter provides that service.

I have devised a quiz to gauge how far along people are in improving their health and lifestyle. This quiz lets you know that you are not alone—that others have suffered as you have, with either similar or completely different results. It allows you to learn about the mistakes you make in exercising that could cause you harm.

The first part of the quiz includes questions about everyday movements and how your body responds to activities such as getting out of bed, not taking a break for lunch, and sitting at a desk for an entire day. The second part of the quiz asks you to evaluate your workouts. Are you sticking to the same routine too long? Are you working the same muscle groups at the beginning of your workouts? Both of these practices make you more susceptible to an injury. I always give this quiz to my patients as part of their overall evaluation. It has been tested time and time again, and people are able to find out for themselves that many of their daily habits are contributing to their back pain and that their exercise workouts are aggravating their condition.

The choices given here represent common situations encountered by people of all fitness levels. You may feel that more than one answer per question applies to you, or you may feel that none apply. Circle the most appropriate choice (or choices). Later, after you are comfortable with a new fitness routine, you can use this quiz as a reference tool to check your progress.

PART 1: EVALUATING YOUR LIFESTYLE

1. When I wake up in the morning, I am:
   a. unable to begin my daily routine immediately
   b. slow to start my routine
   c. able to get out of bed and begin my daily routine immediately
2. When I'm at work, I am aware of:
   a. getting up and moving around frequently in an attempt to relieve stiffness or soreness
   b. making accommodations to my workstation so I am more comfortable
   c. sitting for long periods without discomfort
3. On my lunch break, I:
   a. remain at my workstation
   b. do some type of exercise such as walking or go to the gym
   c. take the opportunity to relax my spine by lying down
4. When I lie down at the end of the day, I am aware of:
   a. spasms in my muscles (particularly in my lower back and legs)
   b. trying to get into a comfortable position
   c. being relaxed and free of pain
5. Regarding involvement in a regular exercise routine or sport, I:
   a. am unable to participate due to pain or lack of flexibility
   b. am dependent on medication to dull pain in order to play
   c. participate fully
6. I exercise at home or go to a gym:
   a. infrequently—two times or less often per week
   b. inconsistently—for a few weeks, stop, and then start up again
   c. regularly—three to five times per week, month after month

PART 2: EVALUATING YOUR EXERCISE ROUTINE

The following questions are designed to be answered by those who exercise regularly. This set of questions will help you evaluate your workouts and exercise patterns to see if you can improve on neglected areas.

7. When I exercise, I:
   a. do only aerobic activities such as walking, running, biking, aerobics, or in-line skating

b. do only weight-training exercises such as with free weights or machines
c. do calisthenics such as push-ups, crunches, yoga, or Pilates
d. combine aerobics, mind and body movements, and weight-training activities

8. I do aerobic activities:
   a. every day
   b. every other day
   c. on the weekend only
9. When I do aerobics, I:
   a. only walk or run
   b. use a device that increases my aerobic intensity such as an elliptical trainer, a bike, or in-line skates, or use a step in an aerobics class
   c. combine the exercises in *a* and *b* in the same workout period
10. I weight-train:
   a. two times per week or less often
   b. more than six times per week
   c. three to four times per week
11. When I work out, I:
   a. use my body weight and calisthenics exercises as a warm-up for my weight-training routine
   b. work with weights one day and do an aerobic activity another day
   c. do weight training and aerobic exercises in the same workout
12. When I do my weight-lifting routine, I:
   a. always do the same exercises in every workout
   b. perform the exercises in the same order each workout
   c. change my routine every week or month
13. When I go to the gym, I:
   a. always warm up for about 20 minutes with steady and light aerobics
   b. hit the weights
   c. climb onto the treadmill or elliptical trainer for my aerobic routine before hitting the weights
14. When I work my chest muscles, I:
   a. always start with the barbell press
   b. use the dumbbell press in my routine at least once a week
   c. use the incline press first in my workout

15. When I work my arms, I:
    a. always start with biceps
    b. use dumbbells and barbells equally in my arm routine
    c. always incorporate cables and machines into my workout
16. When I exercise my back, I:
    a. always do lat pull-downs first
    b. incorporate hyperextension movements into my routine
    c. use equal amounts of rowing movements with pulling exercises in each workout
17. When I work my abdominal muscles, I:
    a. always do the same routine
    b. work them every other day
    c. vary the angles and intensity from one workout to the next
    d. change my abdominal routine for each workout

INTERPRETING YOUR SCORES

Now it's time to tally up your answers and find out how the BackSmart program can help you achieve your fitness goals while eliminating your back and neck pain.

Questions 1–6

If you answered *a* most often for questions 1–6, you have sure signs of spinal problems and need to start the BackSmart program. You are most likely in a stage at which certain movements could unexpectedly aggravate your condition, or you may notice that during the colder months of the year you are less active. You have a greater chance of developing chronic back pain if you do not change your course of action. Your focus should be on the flexibility and strength-training sections of this book.

If you answered *b* most often for questions 1–6, you are most likely in an early stage of developing spinal problems. You try to prevent problems by being more conscious of your body's position at work and at rest. However, you need to act now to prevent any further slide into poor health and pain. Certain everyday movements or occasions of overexertion could exacerbate your condition. Your focus should be on the strengthening and balance sections of this book.

If you answered *c* most often for questions 1–6, you are able to perform a normal routine without signs of spinal problems. You can use the book to tone and shape your body in a safe manner.

Questions 7–17

If you answered *a* or *b* most often, you are likely unable to reach your fitness goals (such as weight loss or toning) because you are performing the same exercises day in and day out. You are overdeveloping certain muscle groups while neglecting others in your workout. This can result in disproportional body parts, which are less appealing and may set you up for injury. You need to utilize different angles in your workouts to enhance the shape of your muscles. Focus on the specialized exercises in the book, such as those to increase flexibility and balance, to give you an athletic look.

If you answered *c* or *d* most often, you are combining your exercises for a well-balanced aerobic and strengthening program. Now you need to reorganize your workouts to improve on your weaknesses first; then you can do your favorite exercises. For example, if you are strong but become winded

AN EYE-OPENING EXPERIENCE

A 49-year-old computer programmer named Mark had played semiprofessional baseball in his early twenties. During that short career playing on the field, he had torn his shoulder and knee ligaments half a dozen times. Mark no longer ran but did ride a bike and use the cross-trainer four or five times per week. He put in long hours in front of the computer and would work through his lunch hour at his desk and then exercise later at night. He complained of stiffness and soreness in his back on and off and thought the problem was due to his sports injuries in the past.

I asked him to take the BackSmart quiz, and afterward he said, "I was shocked to see that not only was I undertraining in many areas, but I was also causing half my problems at my desk at work." It was an eye-opener for Mark to see how some slight changes in his daily routine could improve his appearance and reduce the amount of pain he was feeling from day to day.

easily, you would emphasize aerobic activities first, followed by weights that will help burn fat as well.

Now that you know what your score is, you can begin to make some changes. I recommend that you refer back to the quiz every three to five weeks to make sure you are not sliding back into your old habits. Checking in frequently should keep you on course and help you become successful at achieving your goals.

CHAPTER 2

GROWING PAINS

Let me take you back to a time before my injury and show you my lifestyle, so you can see an example of how pain patterns occur throughout one's life. Then you can see how I accomplished my goals and know that you can accomplish your goals too!

MY STORY

Growing up in the '70s, I played tag, kick the can (my favorite running and agility activity), and, of course, baseball. I was what the gym teachers and coaches called "a natural." I could play any position, throw equally well with both hands, and hit from either side of the plate in baseball. Although I excelled at these team sports, I was bored with their redundancy and predictability. I took up tennis, gymnastics, and diving, which challenged my body further. One summer evening, I went to a drive-in and saw a Bruce Lee movie; I was awed by Bruce Lee's physical ability and martial arts performance. I had been bitten by the martial arts bug, and there was no turning back.

I was in junior high at the time, and I begged and pleaded with my parents to let me try a class at the local karate school. My first, free, introductory lesson with my instructor was memorable. After eventually tying on my pajama-looking sweatpants and belt, I gingerly walked out onto the dojo floor. It was the beginning of a long journey of physical and emotional development for me. I easily moved through the flexibility routine; then came the challenging kicking routine. I knew that I had found the perfect exercise program for me.

I enrolled in beginning classes and began to train seriously at the dojo. We would perform more than seven hundred repetitions of kicks and punching drills in one hour. When I could, I would stay for another hour and a half and repeat the workout, which was usually four out of the five days a week. After only two years of training, I was competing in local state tournaments with athletes twice my age.

Something to Prove

My typical exercise routine Monday through Friday looked like this:

- Go to school and run one to two miles in gym class
- Come home, nap, and then eat a light meal
- Go to the dojo for three hours of free sparring (fighting), calisthenics, board breaking, heavy-bag training, skipping rope, and lots and lots of sit-ups and push-ups on my knuckles (to toughen up the hands, or so they told me)
- Go home again and do homework; eat another meal, and then run one to three miles before falling asleep for the night

On the weekends, I would either practice on my own or run to the house of a friend (about a mile away) and train with him for two or three hours. Then I would run back home. I never took a day off; I was young and in the best shape of my life. When I entered high school, I signed up for an advanced fitness class, which included weight training three times per week and more running. This was the early '80s, when most gym classes consisted of a certain sports activity for one month and then switched to another. Those of us in advanced fitness classes were ahead of our time. We felt like fitness warriors, unstoppable and strong. In the school weight room (really only a cold room inside the field house), there were names on the walls of juniors and seniors who had lifted more than 200, 240, and 250 pounds in the bench press or squat movements. There were no names of freshmen on that wall, and my competitive drive kicked in. I literally fought my way into acceptance in the weight room with the older students. Having a black belt in tae kwon do was beneficial, since I needed to constantly prove my strength and abilities to those older students.

The weight training was just a warm-up for me, because I still had my three-hour martial arts workout and nightly run to finish. I became innovative with my workouts in the weight room, doing exercises no one had ever seen before; I would tie a 45-pound weight around my weight-lifting belt and do dips, push-ups, and chin-ups with the extra weight. The older kids started training with me, but many of them quit because they could not push their bodies as hard. I thought that they just didn't have the mental discipline to see it through.

The weight training helped me to become stronger and faster with my techniques. I had been competing at national tournaments, but now I was winning. Then one day, the football coach called me over and asked if I would like to see my name on the wall for lifting the most weight. Of course, I said I wanted to! Lifting 225 pounds was easy. Then came 240 and 245, and then I felt a pop in my back, which is where my story began.

I didn't want anyone to see how badly I was hurt. I accepted the congratulatory back slapping for being the first freshman to get his name on the wall (right next to my older brother's name). I went to the dojo that night because we were getting ready for a belt promotion and board-breaking demonstration for the public. Being the youngest black belt at the time, I was given one of the more challenging breaks to perform. I had to jump over four kids, bent at their waists, and break four boards at the end. During practice, we used only two boards, and they broke easily. I went home with a sore lower back for the first time in my life. The next morning, I could hardly move; getting out of bed was painful, I had trouble walking upright, and I struggled through the day. When I told my parents I couldn't go to karate, they knew something was seriously wrong. In all the years of doing martial arts, I had never missed a class.

The following day, my parents took me to the pediatrician, who told them that it was a sprained muscle and that I should stop sports and rest in bed. I went home and iced my back for hours and stayed in bed for the entire day. When I got out of bed, I had to crawl on all fours to get to the bathroom; I had no strength to stand up, and the pain was unbearable. My parents took me to a highly respected orthopedist, who did a brief examination and ordered x-rays. We were told that it was a severe sprain. MRI (magnetic resonance imaging) was not commonly used then, but if it had been done, it would have shown a ruptured disk in my spine. The drug of choice was Tylenol with codeine; two weeks' worth of these huge horse pills put me in la-la land, but I was still in pain and could not participate in gym class or any of my exercise programs. Now I was not only in pain but also depressed.

Years of Pain and Frustration

After taking anti-inflammatories and muscle relaxers for a month, I was sent to a physical therapist, who determined that since my flexibility and strength were above normal, he had nothing to offer me! A neurosurgeon told me that I was still young and that time would heal my aches and pains; so he sent me to an occupational therapist, who taught me how to sit and stand properly without causing pain to my back. Only two months earlier, I was running three to five miles a day, but now someone was telling me that my problems would all go away if I just learned to sit and stand correctly. I felt not only frustrated but also angry. She gave me a small, round pillow to place behind my back for support while I was sitting. It was the first time I felt relief from the back pain while sitting. I was encouraged that something placed behind my back made a mechanical correction that would relieve some of my pain.

My dad told me that President John F. Kennedy had suffered from back pain too and that he swam every day. Acting upon my dad's suggestion, I began swimming daily. I built up my endurance to the point that I was able to swim nonstop for one mile, in less than an hour. Although I now felt stronger and had more stamina, I was still in pain when I sat or stood for long periods. After two years of swimming daily, stretching, performing a calisthenics routine, and finally adding back the weight-training exercises, I was almost as strong as before my injury. But martial arts, which was so important to me, was still not a part of my life.

Learning from My Mistakes

A turning point came when I was a premed student and a family friend recommended a sports medicine doctor who used chiropractic care to help athletes. My goal was to return to martial arts and eventually compete again. At the time, this may have seemed like an impossible dream, but I was determined. Progress was slow at first, but I gradually went back to the martial arts and began competing again. I even tried different types of martial arts, from judo to aikido. I developed a routine of challenging exercises and stretches that I continue to perform today. This routine forms the basis of *The BackSmart Fitness Plan.*

My struggle to overcome my back pain, combined with the relief I ultimately obtained through the combination of exercise and chiropractic care, caused me to rethink what type of doctor I wanted to become. When I realized that I could become a doctor who helps people lessen their pain, without the use of surgery or drugs, I made the decision to become a doctor of chiropractic medicine. During my residency rotation, I took my patients to the rehabilitation room and showed them how to execute my exercises, and I saw that they were getting better. I was ecstatic! I knew I had found a strong foundation for the care of back-pain sufferers who still wanted to work out and enhance their strength and flexibility. When I opened my practice, I was the only doctor in my area with a weight room in the office, offering classes to the public. In my BackSmart seminars, I offer people a method of exercise to help them achieve their health and fitness goals.

I understand how my patients feel when they walk through the door; I've been there myself. I have helped my patients who have neck and back pain return to a normal active lifestyle, and now I hope that readers of this book will use my method of exercise to achieve their fitness and health goals.

CHAPTER 3

KEYS TO A SUCCESSFUL WORKOUT

The soul of the workout is to do no harm to the body. But be prepared to have challenging, effective, and fun workouts you never thought possible. Before going through the exercises in Part 2, I've laid out a few ground rules.

I have chosen the routines in this book based on more than 20 years of experience training people of different skill levels, ages, shapes, and sizes, from professional and Olympic athletes to overweight, stressed-out folks who have not exercised since childhood. All of them have succeeded with the BackSmart program by following these guidelines. By using this system, you can achieve your goals as well and get into the best shape of your life.

In Chapter 9, you can choose the basic program for the first 6 to 10 weeks of training and then move to the intermediate level, which is more challenging. Or you can use any combination of the various routines for the best results.

STEPS TO KEEP YOU ON TRACK

There are plenty of ways to eat right and exercise, and you probably know most of them. So, why is it so hard to start, or stick with, a diet and workout plan? Perhaps what's missing is motivation, that mysterious ingredient that helps you do what you promised yourself you would do.

Those who succeed with a healthy lifestyle don't have more willpower; they just know how to make a habit seductive enough so that it pulls on them, rather than their having to push it. Maximize your motivation with these smart steps. You'll stay on track and keep on progressing—success is practically guaranteed.

1. **Mix it up.** If you are occasionally uninspired or feel as if you hit a plateau, try alternating the intensity of your workout, or do the Tuesday workout two days in a row, or switch Friday's workout to the beginning of the week. This will not only force your body to adapt but also keep you fresh and have you looking forward to a challenge in your workout as you burn more calories and stimulate muscle growth. Another method is to switch from weight machines to free-weight-only workouts from time to time.

2. **Chart your progress.** Those who are successful in creating a healthy habit map out the exact details of their exercise routine and what days they are going to do specific activities. Keeping a written track of your fitness routine and your progress can be one of the most effective ways to lose weight and stick with an exercise program. Knowing how far you went and how fast you walked, how many calories you burned, and how intensely you're working can be an excellent motivator, especially if you're seeing improvements in your performance. Along the way, you can adjust and set new goals and can even pull back if you find yourself pushing too hard.

3. **Create a compelling atmosphere.** To make exercise more fun, find a location in which you'll feel comfortable and that is easily accessible, choose a time that suits you, and take your workout clothes with you to work or leave an extra bag in your car.

4. **Prioritize.** Put your health at the top of your to-do list. It takes at least three to four weeks to lock in to a new habit. For this new month, hone your new lifestyle so that exercise becomes more habit-forming than watching TV or doing something else. Try to work out daily by making exercise a ritual, and avoid taking two consecutive days off. People who work out just once or twice a week are more likely to fall off the exercise wagon than those who exercise three or four times per week. That's because consistency has a greater effect than the duration of the workout or what you do in that session. If you can only squeeze in a few minutes here and there, spread them out over the week to sustain your

momentum. This will enhance your habit-forming behavior, and your mind and body will begin to crave it.

5. **Schedule exercise appointments.** Leave notes on your doors, mirrors, car dashboard, and computer to remind you of the results of a regular workout routine. A habit starts when you do the same thing at the same time almost every day, no excuses. When establishing a pattern, for example, make that treadmill session as important as meeting with your friends. Research has shown that morning exercisers may be slightly more successful than afternoon or evening exercisers because they're finished before distractions and fatigue set in. But stick to the time that works best for you.

6. **Daily dose.** If you're strapped for time, keep your mind and body in the exercise groove by squeezing in a few movements from the wall exercises or the BackSmart Daily Dozen stretches (Chapter 4). Working your abdominals daily (Chapter 5) will enhance your muscle memory while burning calories rather than storing them as fat if you choose not to do your complete workout. Take small steps and you will get better results. It's also good to identify the scenarios that might derail your routine—such as trips, holidays, and work deadlines—and prepare a backup plan. Have an alternative workout strategy, and be ready with a solution for your potential detours from fitness so that whenever you hit a roadblock, you'll know how to overcome it. Above all, try to avoid adopting an all-or-nothing attitude. As an example, you could perform the balance drills (Chapter 6) and the BackSmart Daily Dozen wherever you are.

7. **Visualize.** Mentally review your plans. Cut out images of fit people from fitness magazines and tell yourself that is your goal. Visualize yourself doing the exercises before your workout starts. Focus on how your muscles look as you do the exercises in your mind; this will help you overcome any mental barriers you may have regarding the amount of weight you are using on a given exercise or the number of repetitions to be performed.

8. **Aim high.** Whether you want to increase your endurance, lose weight, participate in your first triathlon, or lift a certain amount of weight before your birthday, having something to work toward is a surefire way to keep

you going. Have a short-term, specific, and realistic goal in mind. For example, "I will walk and stretch for 20 minutes every day," versus "I will lose weight and exercise more." When you find yourself meeting goals with ease, set more challenging ones. Use the training log in Chapter 9 to record your long-term and short-term goals.

9. **Reward yourself.** Surveys have shown that people who reward themselves are two to three times more likely to meet their goals than peo-

---

USING THE KEY STEPS FOR POSITIVE RESULTS

Nicole, a 39-year-old nurse, came to see me due to an injury she sustained while at the gym. She had been training with weights for years and had thought she may have hurt herself early in the day before going to the gym and hoped her workout would help. When she went for her morning walk, she had strained her lower back, but thought she could walk it out because she had usually felt better after her workouts. Unfortunately, that was not the case this time. She also said she felt stale from her workouts, and because she didn't want to bulk up, she would never increase the weights or do more repetitions.

I asked her if she ever rewarded herself for working out every session she had planned for the month. She said she never really looked at it that way; she knew it was good for her, so she basically showed up and did her thing and left. She was setting herself up for future injuries with this attitude, and so I asked her to write down two goals, be they physical accomplishments in the gym, weight loss, or whatever else she felt would motivate her. I told her to visualize herself working out before she went to the gym. After completing each workout, she would place a star or draw a smiley face on her calendar next to the date she'd worked out, thus reinforcing her commitment to herself in a positive way.

After one month, we followed up, and Nicole told me she had not only lost weight but also felt more self-confident when she went into the gym because she saw herself doing the movements beforehand and now knew she could bypass her previous mental barrier. As a result of using the Back-Smart program, she feels more motivated and has fewer aches and pains.

---

ple who don't give themselves any reward for their accomplishments. Buy yourself some new clothes or a music CD, or treat yourself to a day at the spa or a sporting event.

10. **Celebrate success.** All the little victories bring you closer to your overall goal and are a realistic way to achieve your goals. Don't expect to nail the perfect workout or desired body weight overnight. The acquisition stage lasts 30 to 60 days. Plan for these milestones by writing them in on your calendar, and they will be here before you know it.

THE BASIC TRAINING PRINCIPLES

It takes hard, dedicated work to build your ideal physique, but hard work alone is not enough. You also need knowledge and a mastery of principles that make your training effective. These fundamental principles should be learned and adopted right from the beginning. It is much easier to learn the proper way to do something than it is to unlearn the wrong way and have to start over.

Warming Up

Often when people talk about "warming up," they don't understand how literally that should be taken. When you use a muscle, the temperature in the area actually rises, allowing you to contract the muscle more forcefully. This makes it possible to train more intensely and to derive more benefit from your workout.

Warming up also pumps fresh, oxygenated blood to the area and increases the heart rate. This provides maximum oxygen supply to your body and helps to eliminate the waste products of the exercise from the working muscles.

Finally, warming up properly helps to protect your body from becoming overstressed, prepares it for the demands of training, and reduces the chance of injury, such as a sprain or strain.

For each different exercise during your workout, you begin with one light warm-up set in order to get those specific muscles ready to do that specific movement. The time of day is also a factor in determining how much warming up you need. If you are training at eight o'clock in the morning, you are likely to be tighter and more in need of stretching and warming up than you are at eight at night, so adjust your preliminaries accordingly.

Always take care that you warm up thoroughly. Injuries in the gym happen for two primary reasons: either sloppy technique (such as too much weight or failing to keep the weights under control) or failure to stretch or warm up properly.

Completing Sets

Generally, the basic training program I recommend is doing two to three sets of each exercise, except where otherwise specified. I believe this is the best system, for several reasons:

1. You need to do at least two to three sets in order to have the volume of training necessary to fully stimulate all available muscle fiber. But if you do more sets per exercise, your total training by volume will be so great that you'll risk overtraining.

2. Doing two to three sets per exercise in the basic training program and four to five sets in advanced training enables you to do a sufficient variety of exercises to work all the areas of a body part—upper and lower back, for example.

3. The experience of my two decades of training has proven that the maximum amount of weight you can handle that allows you to just make it through two to three sets of an exercise will stimulate the muscles sufficiently.

For smaller muscle groups such as the biceps and triceps, you actually need fewer total sets, as the arms get a lot of incidental training when you work the other areas of the upper body.

Completing Repetitions Within Sets

To get the most out of the training, unless otherwise specified, you should train to failure in each set. This simply means you should continue doing your repetitions until you are unable to lift the weight anymore. This ensures that you stimulate as much muscle fiber as possible.

But you don't go on indefinitely when training to failure. Instead, you choose the weight for the exercise that will cause you to fail at or near a specific number of repetitions. For example:

- **First set.** Choose a weight that causes you to fail at about 15 repetitions. This serves as a warm-up set.
- **Second set.** Increase the weight so that you fail at about 12 repetitions.
- **Third set.** Increase the weight again so that you fail at about 10 repetitions.

Training this way gives you the best of all possible worlds: you start out relatively light, which gives your muscles time to fully warm up for the particular exercise; you go on to do slightly fewer repetitions with a heavier weight, which forces lots of blood into the muscles; and finally you add on more weight so that you are training relatively heavy for strength.

Progressive Resistance

Your muscles will grow only when they are subject to an overload. They will not respond to anything less. As you grow stronger, the only way to make your muscles continue to grow is by increasing the amount of work you force them to do.

This is most easily done by increasing the amount of weight used in each exercise. By progressively adding on weight to keep pace with the growing strength of your body, you ensure that your muscles will always be working at their maximum capacity and therefore will grow as fast as possible.

Full Range of Motion

Except for specialized partial-range movements, your exercises should take any muscle through its longest possible range of motion. You should take care to stretch out to the full extension and then come all the way back to a position of complete contraction. This is the only way to stimulate the entire muscle and every muscle fiber.

Choosing the Right Weights

The idea of training, unless you are doing heavy lifts or power training for a special purpose, is not to lift too heavy or too light. If you lift too heavy, you will tend to cheat—you won't work through a full range of motion and can't do enough repetitions; too light, and you will not put sufficient stress on the muscle to make it grow.

Occasionally you will use an amount of weight for an exercise that would normally make you fail at 10 repetitions, but you will feel exceptionally strong and be able to grind out 12 or 13 repetitions instead. That's fine; keep going as long as you can and in any set. Don't stop simply because you have arrived at a certain number.

But the opposite will happen from time to time, and you will be able to do only 8 repetitions with a weight you usually handle for 10. As long as you continue to go to failure, you are still getting the most out of your training even though your body may not be as powerful on that particular day.

If, however, you are doing your set and you find yourself continuing on to do 13, 15, or more repetitions, you will know that you need to use more weight on that exercise. So, for the next set, you would increase the weight so that your repetitions return to the specific guidelines.

Resting Between Sets

It is important to pace yourself properly through a workout. If you try to train too fast, you risk overloading the cardiovascular system before you have worked the muscles sufficiently. Also, you may have a tendency to get sloppy and start throwing the weights around instead of executing each movement correctly.

However, training too slowly is bad too. If you take five minutes between each set, your heart rate slows down, your muscles get cold, and your level of intensity drops to nothing.

Try to keep your rest periods between sets to a minute or less. In the first minute after weight-training exercise, you recover 70 percent of your strength, and by three minutes, you have recovered all you are going to recover without extended rest.

Remember that the point of this training is to stimulate and fatigue the maximum amount of muscle fiber possible, and this happens only when the body is forced to recruit additional muscle fiber to replace what is fatigued. So, you don't want to allow your muscles to recover too much between sets—just enough to be able to continue your workout and to keep forcing the body to innervate more and more muscle tissue.

There is one other factor to consider. Physiologists have long noted the link between maximum muscle strength and muscular endurance. The stronger you are, the more times you can lift a submaximal amount of weight. This means that the more you press yourself to develop muscular (as opposed to cardiovascular) endurance, the stronger you will become. So, maintaining a regular pace in your training actually leads to an increase in overall strength.

Order of Exercises

I have experimented with all the different types of exercises and movements, adapting them for the various shapes, sizes, and fitness levels of my patients over the years. I found that the most important aspect of training was not which exercises they performed but rather in which order they did them.

New exercisers tend to ignore the development of their legs, concentrating instead on the arms and torso. Such a lopsided program will permit injuries to occur as a result of poor planning. If you start out with the smaller muscle groups and then move to the larger muscles, you will be weaker and may cause yourself injury. On the other hand, if you work all your larger muscle groups at the beginning of your workout, you will use up most of your energy and have nothing left for the rest of your workout.

It is important to follow the order I have suggested in the chapters, especially for the flexibility routine and core training. By working your muscles through the given movements, you are building on the previous one performed, thus enhancing the quality of your workout and following these basic principles:

- For maximum exercise, the training program must be well rounded and must include exercises for each of the major body parts.
- The greatest concentration should be directed toward working the largest muscles in the body.
- The exercise sequence should be arranged so the muscles are worked in the order of the relative sizes, from the largest to smallest.

In practice, this last point prescribes that the lower body be worked before the upper body. As a rule, your thighs are exercised before the calves, the back before the chest, and the upper arms before the forearms. Since the waist muscles are used to stabilize the upper body in most exercises, they should be worked after the upper-body movements.

WHAT TO DO IF YOU FEEL STRAIN: OVERTRAINING AND RECUPERATION

Intensity is the measure of how hard you force the muscles to work in any training session. The more work you do in any given period, the more intensely you train. However, the more intense your workouts, the more recuperation time your body needs in order to rest and grow.

Overtraining occurs when you work a muscle too often to allow it to fully recuperate. You hear die-hard weight lifters talk about "tearing the muscle down" and then letting it rebuild itself, but this is not really physiologically accurate. There can be small amounts of tissue damage during heavy exercise, and it is this damage that is associated with residual muscular soreness.

A number of complex biochemical processes accompany strenuous muscular contraction. Muscular contraction results in the buildup of toxic waste products such as lactic acid, a natural body response—but it slows the body down, causing tightness and muscle aches while your body heals itself. The body requires time to restore the chemical balance of the muscle cells, to clear out the residual waste products, and to restock the depleted stores of glycogen. Time is also needed for the cells themselves to adapt to the stimulus of the exercise—and to grow. After all, that's what training is all about, making muscles grow. So, if you overtrain a muscle, forcing it to work too hard too quickly after the preceding exercise session, you will not give it a chance to grow, and your progress will slow.

Different muscles recover from exercise at different rates. The arms, for example, recover the fastest. The lower-back muscles recover the slowest, in order to completely recuperate from a workout. In most cases, giving each body part 48 hours of rest is sufficient, which means skipping a day after training a muscle before training it again.

Basic training involves only medium levels of intensity, so the time necessary for recuperation is shorter. Once you move on to more advanced training, higher levels of intensity will be needed in order to overcome the greater resistance of the body to change and grow. However, trained muscles recover from fatigue faster than untrained muscles, so the better you get at exercising, the faster your recovery rate will be and the more intense your training program can become.

The key to a successful workout when exercising is to periodically vary your workouts. This way, as soon as your body starts adapting to what you are doing, you progressively intensify the program and avoid these unwanted sticking points. By following these programs as outlined in the basic, intermediate, and advanced levels, you'll be able to do just that.

INTERRUPTING YOUR TRAINING

What happens when you stop training? This is a question I am frequently asked.

Sometimes it is necessary to stop for a while. If you are feeling very tired and sore, you may be overtraining. Take a one- to three-day break and then resume normal training to the point where you left off. Or if you are forced to take a few weeks off because of work or family obligations, start back on an easier program.

If you take more than one week off before you finish the basic program, then start again at the beginning. The longer the time period when you're not training, the more likely it is that you will return to the condition you were in before you started. Muscles do not and cannot turn into fat, because they are a different type of tissue. However, when you stop exercising but keep the same routine as when you were exercising, you may gain weight because the extra calories and carbohydrates are not being burned off.

EVERY BREATH YOU TAKE

This section explores breathing techniques that can be performed to reduce back pain and to speed recovery after workouts by lowering the heart rate and relaxing the muscles, thus eliminating fatigue. This information will also help you if you are among those who suffer from acute back pain and say that everything—even breathing—causes you pain. You will find that these breathing exercises will help you build confidence while relaxing the deep muscles wrapped around the rib cage and spine.

Breathing Incorrectly

Most people breathe incorrectly while working out, causing undue stress and tension throughout the body, sapping their energy and strength. Many are hyperventilating after each repetition; they are probably "getting a buzz" out of their workouts because they don't have enough oxygen going up to the brain! (Slow and deliberate breathing is required from the diaphragm, not the upper chest.) Others are notorious breath holders. These people turn red in the face, not from exertion but because of the buildup in blood pressure in the head! These common problems can be corrected by practicing proper breathing exercises.

Breathing Correctly

You breathe 24 hours a day without having to think about it. Often your breath intake is at a bare minimum. Taking time to concentrate and breathe more fully is well worth it. This practice can change your state of mind from stressed to serene. The breath is the link between the body and mind. When the breath becomes steady and flows freely, agitation melts away and you feel a relaxed inner steadiness.

Proper breathing depends on eliminating tension plus correcting bad habits and wrong mental and physical attitudes. The moment you rid yourself of these obstacles, your breathing will come into its own and bring you vitality and good health.

There are three separate forms of breathing: diaphragmatic (from the diaphragm and abdominal region), intercostal (from the middle section of the lungs), and clavicular (from the upper part of the lungs). Complete breathing combines all three and constitutes the ideal technique.

Complete Respiration

Complete respiration integrates all three methods into one single, full, rhythmic movement. It is best done on your back, following these steps:

1. Empty the lungs entirely.
2. Slowly lower the diaphragm, allowing air to enter the lungs when the abdomen swells, filling the bottom half of the lungs with air.
3. Expand the ribs without straining.
4. Allow the lungs to completely fill by raising the shoulders and collarbone.

Throughout this procedure, the air should enter in a continuous flow, without gasps. There should be no noise; it is essential to breathe silently. When the lungs are completely filled, breathe out, using the same sequence as when inhaling. Now breathe in again in the same way; you may continue for as long as you wish. This process should not induce any discomfort or fatigue.

You can practice this breathing at any time of the day, whenever you think of it, wherever you are; whether at work or at home or while walking or driving, just breathe consciously and as completely as possible. Gradually you will acquire the habit of complete respiration, and your method of breathing will improve as you go on. It is essential to reserve a few minutes of practice every day, a special time that is convenient for you. In the morning when you wake up is a good time, and so is the evening before going to sleep.

Inhalation, like exhalation, must be silent. Do not blow yourself up like a balloon! Breathe easily without straining; remember that the ideal respiration is deep, slow, silent, and easy.

Working with Your Body's Natural Rhythm

You must learn to let nature take its course. Your body knows to breathe faster when you work harder, and your body doesn't need help when you are sleeping. Without your mind even thinking about it, your body will take care of itself. Overbreathing, or hyperventilation, actually starves the body and brain of something they need more than oxygen, and that is carbon dioxide. So, when you begin a weight-training movement, remember that you are not going for a world record! Instead, remember to breathe in through your nose and out through your mouth during repetitions. Keep in mind that deep breathing is healthy and that shallow breathing reduces your strength.

At the end of your workout, sit down; note the number of breaths you are taking and your pulse rate. Now slowly take a deep breath, hold it for two seconds, and then breathe out through your mouth. Repeat this sequence for 20 repetitions, and then relax into normal breathing for two minutes. Check your breathing and pulse again; both rates should be lower. If they're not, repeat the sequence for another 20 repetitions. Once you are breathing more slowly and your pulse rate is down, stretch out and drink plenty of water. By performing this procedure after your workouts, you will lower your heart rate and improve your recovery time.

When you practice these breathing exercises, you will not only reduce your aches and pains but also speed up your recovery time after your workouts. As you do the breathing exercises, your confidence will continue to build and you will feel more relaxed by correctly breathing during your workouts, effectively melting away the stress and tension throughout your body.

INCORPORATING MUSIC

I discovered the use of music early on in my practice, when the 12- to 15-hour days I worked were taking a toll on me. I felt little energy at the end of the day, and even though I adjusted my diet and increased my exercise, I still felt drained when five o'clock rolled around. Then I began to play CDs that were mostly instrumental, and I developed a groove. I felt emotionally uplifted and more positive.

When patients walk into my center, they are met neither by silence nor by pop radio stations repeating the same music over and over. Instead, they are greeted by the rhythmic sounds of a flamenco guitar or an infusion of Latin jazz. Depending on the given day, they might even hear classical music or a New Age mix. Different, you say? Notice how long you wait in most doctors' offices and how easy it is to become bored and angry. On the other hand, patients waiting in my center enjoy the music, which helps put them in a relaxed state.

Studies have found that certain types of music slow the breathing patterns and lower the heart rates of listeners. It has been shown that brain waves can be altered by music. Music can also motivate you, improve your learning curve, and enhance your test performance. Most important, it can help to reduce stress and decrease pain.

Start your day with some uplifting music before and during your morning workouts. Later in the day, switch to a more upbeat rhythm to maintain alertness and to continue your energy drive for your evening workout. Instead of watching television at night, listen to some form of relaxing music while reading or stretching.

Remember to use these key principles in your workouts and you will achieve your ideal athletic body without the typical aches and pains along the way. And your workouts will help prevent future injuries due to poor workout habits.

PART 2

Exercising the Healthy Body

CHAPTER 4

INCREASE YOUR FLEXIBILITY WITH BACKSMART STRETCHING

Remember that Rome wasn't built in a day. Patience and persistence are vital for accomplishing any worthwhile endeavor. Time and again, I come across former patients whom I haven't seen in years, and they stop to tell me how wonderful they feel and how the BackSmart Daily Dozen contributes to their relief and success in not having relapses of back pain.

BENEFITS OF STRETCHING

Start off each day with these warm-up exercises, which will enhance your mobility and longevity of movement throughout the day. Warm-up movements in the morning are necessary to improve muscle elasticity, reduce stress to joints, and prepare the body for the rest of the day's activities.

The stretches described in this chapter will help reduce your muscular aches and pains that are associated with performing everyday activities. They will help improve your posture and release muscle tension, with the added benefit of stress reduction. Joint pain and stiffness will be minimized, because the increase in flexibility allows your joints and muscles to move more freely, resulting in greater range of motion.

Three Keys to Stretching

No matter how intent you are on learning the finer points of stretching, you are unlikely to achieve your ultimate goals unless you incorporate these three important techniques:

1. **Maintain a solid lower-back position.** While stretching, keep your lower back in its natural position, neither rounded nor straight as a board. Regardless of the body part on which you are focusing, remember to maintain your lower-back position—when you are standing, lying, or sitting. You can achieve much more flexibility by maintaining a proper lower-back position.

2. **Concentrate on the area that you are stretching.** When you focus your attention on the specific muscles that you are attempting to stretch, your muscles will relax, and you will feel the difference. Simply go as far as you can, take your time, and hold the position.

3. **Remember to breathe.** As you breathe, oxygen is carried through your body and into your muscles, allowing you to stretch to your maximum level. Be sure to inhale through your nose and exhale through your mouth.

What Not to Do When Stretching

Just as it's important to keep the three preceding points in mind, it's also important to know what not to do when stretching. Certain actions in particular should be avoided:

- Do not round your back. For example, when people perform the classic leg stretch, they typically attempt to touch their toes with their hands. Most people round their backs, which decreases the effect of the stretch.

- Be careful not to bounce or jerk while holding a stretch, as this may lead to an injury.

- Do not hold your breath, as your muscles will become tense. Breathing slowly and deeply will help you relax and increase flexibility.

STARTING YOUR WARM-UP SLOWLY

Susan, a 38-year-old mother of two, first came to see me right after giving birth to her first child. She had lost the weight she had gained during her pregnancy quite easily, but her lower and middle back had been bothering her ever since. She'd tried all those standard back exercises done lying on her back but was disappointed with her results. She worried that she was stuck with this pain forever and would not be able to return to her regular exercise routine.

I started her off slowly with the first half of the BackSmart Daily Dozen stretches, having her perform half the number of repetitions until she felt ready for more.

She reported: "When I first started these stretches, I thought I would never be able to reach beyond my toes or bend my body in that manner. But in a matter of weeks, I started to relax into the stretches, and they became easier to do. It's been four months, and my back pain has diminished, and I started the BackSmart weight-training part this week. I feel I have more energy now and less pain than when I started."

What helped Susan and many others like her was using the active range-of-motion stretches to enhance her flexibility with minimum effort. No longer was she trying to touch her toes or hold certain stretch positions for what seemed like endless minutes; instead, she glided from one stretch to the next, improving her overall muscle elasticity and agility.

THE BACKSMART DAILY DOZEN

These movements can be done anywhere and as often as needed throughout the day. You can also use them as a warm-down before retiring for the night. I created this series of exercises because I needed to change the angles to allow a more flowing motion, enabling you to move easily from one movement to the next. I began to develop a rhythmic, smooth glide into the positions, thus preventing resistance and pain.

If you experience any sharp pain while performing any of these or other stretches, evaluate your body position. Focus on the key points listed in the earlier section, and this will usually resolve your problem. If not, start with the wall stretches later in this chapter, and do them until you feel comfortable enough to move to the BackSmart Daily Dozen.

For each exercise, I instruct you to complete a number of *sets* (a set comprises the whole movement) for a number of times (*repetitions*). I may also instruct you to hold the position for a number of seconds, depending on your level.

A Flexibility Exercise to Determine Your Level

First I'd like you to do a simple flexibility exercise to determine which of three levels would be appropriate for you at this stage. Sit on the floor with your legs outstretched in front of you while reaching with both hands toward your feet. If you have to place your hands behind you for support due to tightness in your legs and lower back, you should start off at the beginner level. If you can reach your hands to your knees, start with the intermediate level. If you can touch your ankles or toes, start at the advanced level. You can also use this guideline to gauge your progress and to judge when you are able to move up to the next level.

After completing the first four stretches, refer to the following list to determine out how many sets and reps you should complete for the rest of the BackSmart Daily Dozen stretches.

- **Beginner.** 4 sets of 10 repetitions, holding the stretch for 5 seconds.
- **Intermediate.** 4 to 6 sets of 10 repetitions, holding the stretch for 5 to 10 seconds.
- **Advanced.** 6 to 8 sets of 10 repetitions, holding the stretch for 10 seconds to a minute.

1. Arm Circles

This movement relaxes the muscles between the spine and shoulder blades, warms up the shoulder joints, and brings circulation to the shoulder muscles.

1. Start with your arms out to the sides at shoulder height.

2. Move your arms backward in small circles, gradually building to wider circles and reaching upward as high as possible.

3. Rise up on your toes each time you make a circle, to warm up your calves and feet. (Be careful not to whip your arms around too quickly, as this can tear fibers in the rotator cuffs—the muscles that hold the shoulders in their sockets.)

4. Start slowly, relax into the movement, and concentrate on the stretch that you feel at the top of the movement and when you bring your arms back behind you.

5. Complete 2 to 4 sets of 20 to 30 circles, and then change direction and circle forward.

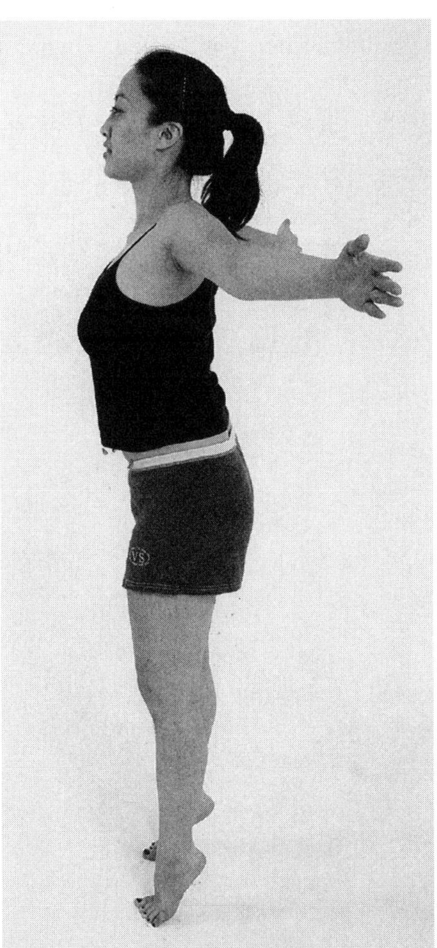

Photo 4.1
Arm Circles

2. Wrist and Elbow Circles

Using movements not normally done in everyday activities, wrist and elbow circles relax the muscles around the wrist and elbow joints.

1. Start by flexing and relaxing your fingers and shaking out your hands.

2. Slowly and then vigorously, move your wrists clockwise in small circles, with the fingers flexed upward.

3. Perform 2 to 4 sets of 20 to 30 repetitions, and then move the wrists counterclockwise.

4. Repeat this exercise making circles with your elbows, bending them and with your hands pointed either down or out at your sides.

5. Perform 2 to 4 sets of 20 to 30 circles, first clockwise and then counterclockwise.

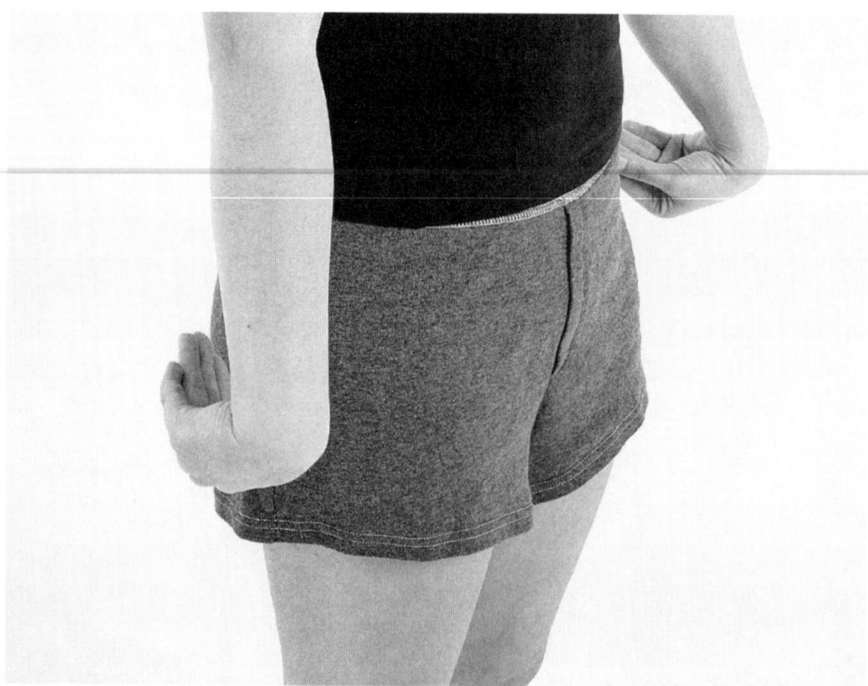

Photo 4.2
Wrist Circles

3. Neck Circles

The next two exercises can easily be done while you're sitting at a desk.

With the neck circles, the layers of neck muscles that support the head, which are typically tightened from sitting at a desk too long, are relaxed.

1. Begin with your head straight.
2. Drop your chin to your chest, and slowly move your head in small circles to the right, gradually building to larger circles. (Do not move in the up-and-down manner commonly done on aerobic tapes, as that movement can cause whiplash.)
3. Complete 2 to 4 sets of 10 to 20 circles in each direction.

4. Shoulder Shrugs

This simple movement easily relaxes the large trapezius muscle group.

1. Raise your shoulders toward your ears for the first few repetitions.
2. Gradually rotate your shoulders backward at the top of the movement and then down.
3. Repeat this movement and feel the stretch in the upper-back muscles as you bring your arms back and down. (Keep your hands relaxed throughout the exercise.)
4. Complete 2 to 4 sets of 10 to 20 repetitions.

5. The Sail

Refer to the flexibility exercise earlier in this chapter to establish the appropriate level for you in performing the rest of these stretches. The list in that section tells you how many sets and reps to complete as well as how long to hold each stretch.

The sail prepares you for other stretches, by working the lower body as well as the upper-back muscles. While doing this exercise, I visualize myself as a sail catching the wind, holding steady as I lift my chest and lengthen my arms, and slowly relaxing my back muscles. Thus, the name of the stretch.

1. Sit on the floor, with your left leg stretched out in front of you and the foot flexed, with toes pointing up. (Your leg should not be relaxed with a bent knee or with your foot hanging lazily over to the side.) Bend your right leg so that your right foot is touching the inside of your left thigh.

2. Sit tall, with shoulders relaxed and squared. Hold in your stomach as you breathe in and out deeply. With the arm straight, place your right hand on your right knee, keeping your shoulders relaxed.

3. Slowly press your right knee toward the floor, if it is not already there. (You should feel a stretch on the right side of your body—at your leg, hip, and upper back and underneath your right arm.)

4. Extend your left arm and slide your hand along your left leg until you reach your foot.

Photo 4.3
The Sail

5. With your left hand, hold your toes in a pulled-back position, feeling the stretch throughout the entire back of your calf, hamstrings, buttocks, and lower-back region.

6. Hold this position for a count of 5 to 60 seconds, and then relax to the neutral position, with both arms down in front of your waist.

7. Repeat the stretch with your right leg out in front and your left leg bent.

Key Points to Remember

- Depending on your flexibility, you may not be able to reach your foot immediately in step 4. Don't push yourself! Perform the stretch reaching only to a position that is comfortable—perhaps your calf at first and eventually your ankle.

- As you should for all the stretches, keep good form: do not bounce and do not cave in your lower back.

- Be sure to relax your shoulders and upper back while bending forward.

- While stretching, remember to breathe deeply and fully—in through the nose and out through the mouth. Many of us forget to breathe while exercising, causing the body to tighten up, which is the opposite of what we are trying to accomplish.

6. Swim Stretch

After the sail stretch, your body should be ready for stretching that is more active. The swim stretch combines a series of movements. This stretch builds endurance and improves range of motion and flexibility in the neck, back, shoulder, and leg muscles all at once. It is an effective stretch when you are short on time and want to relax stiff postural muscles.

1. Start this stretch in the same position as you did for the sail. (Reach out with your left hand and grab your calf, ankle, or foot, depending on your

flexibility, and hold this position. Turn your body so that your left shoulder points forward and your right shoulder points back.)

2. Relax and place the left side of your face on your left shoulder (as if you are taking a breath during a freestyle stroke).
3. Reach back as far as you can with your right hand. (Visualize a relay runner waiting to accept the baton during a handoff.)
4. Rotate your arm upward, reaching as high as possible, then slowly bring your arm forward toward your leg. Keep your arm close enough to your head to touch your right ear. (You should feel the back and shoulder muscles stretch and release.)
5. Try to touch the little toe on your left foot.
6. Pull your right arm back immediately, and start the stretch again.
7. Repeat the stretch with your right leg out in front and your left leg bent.

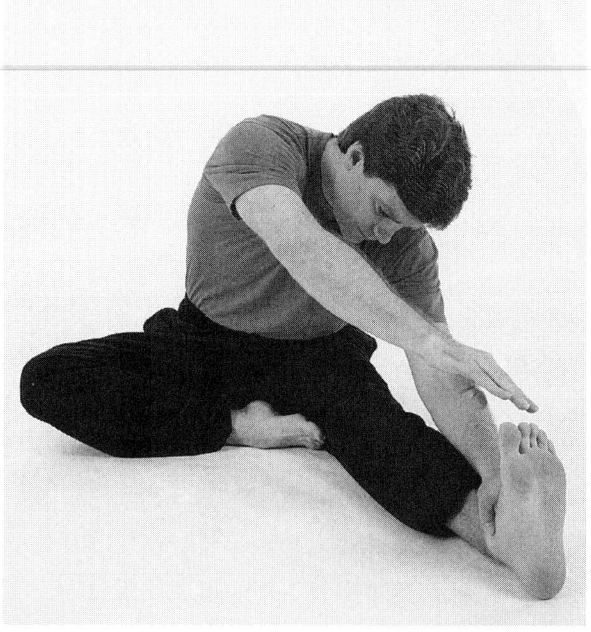

Photo 4.4
Swim Stretch

Key Points to Remember

- Keep your head down, resting on your shoulder, and relax your body forward during the entire stretch.

- Be sure to reach far enough and high enough so that the shoulder and upper-back muscle groups release.

7. Swan Dive Stretch

This stretch should be performed after the swim stretch and is done in two parts to give you the full benefit of unlocking your body's tightness and enhance the circulation into the muscle groups being stretched. While the swan dive is predominantly a stretching movement, by supporting your weight with your arms, you also strengthen your upper body.

First Movement

1. While still sitting on the floor, place both legs out in front of your body, with toes pointing up. (Remember to sit up tall with shoulders squared, breathe deeply, and tighten your stomach muscles.)

2. Reach forward with both hands over your feet, not down toward them.

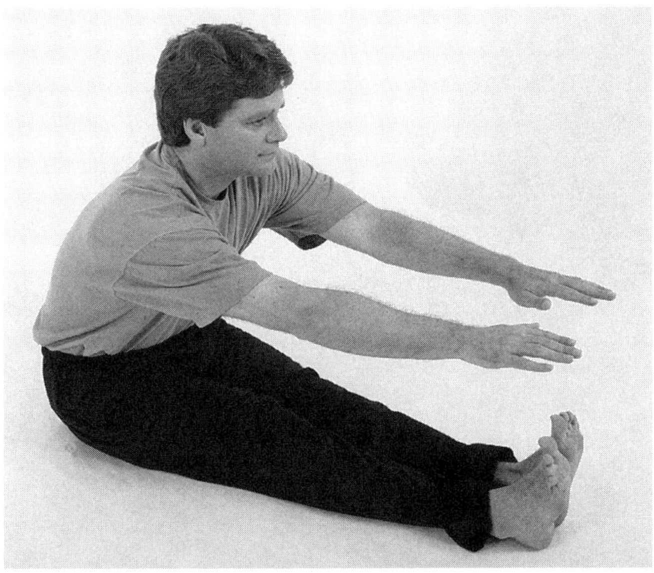

Photo 4.5
Swan Dive Stretch (first movement)

3. Flex your toes back as you lean forward, feeling the stretch in the calves, hamstrings, buttocks, and lower back. (You should feel the pull behind your shoulder and upper-back muscles.)

4. Hold this position for 5 to 10 seconds, lifting your chest, with your back straight and shoulders relaxed.

Second Movement

1. Slowly sit up as you move your arms out and back behind you at shoulder level (as if doing a breaststroke movement).

2. Place your hands behind you on the floor, with fingers pointing toward your back.

3. Slowly lift your chest, dropping your head back just enough to feel the stretch in your chest and neck.

4. Raise up on your heels, so that your legs are off the floor. (Be sure to keep your back straight—do not arch your back or bend at the waist.)

Photo 4.6
Swan Dive Stretch (second movement)

5. Hold this position for 5 to 10 seconds, and then slowly lower yourself to the sitting position and immediately reach your hands forward, repeating the entire exercise.

For a Challenge

In step 2 of the second movement, you can place your fingers pointing away from your body to increase the stretch in your arms and chest.

Key Points to Remember

- For the first part of the movement, stretch forward, not down, as you relax your fingers and wrists.
- You are starting what I call "active stretching"—moving your body during stretches while working opposing muscle groups in a rhythmic and controlled fashion.
- Do not jerk your body forward or upward using pure muscle strength to achieve the end positions, as you will end up with pulled muscle groups.

8. Side-Kick Stretch

The side-kick stretch, which has three distinct arm movements, releases the deep tissue fibers along the lower back and waist, giving you a greater range of motion. This movement may feel awkward at first if you have tightness in your hip flexors or lower back, but you'll be fine as long as you relax and bend smoothly and gently downward.

First Movement

1. Stretch your left leg out to the side, with the left (outer) side of the foot facing up and the right (inner) side resting on the floor. The knee should be locked. Bend your right leg so that your right foot is touching the inside of your left thigh.
2. Reach out toward your left leg with your left hand, while pressing your right hand on your right knee.

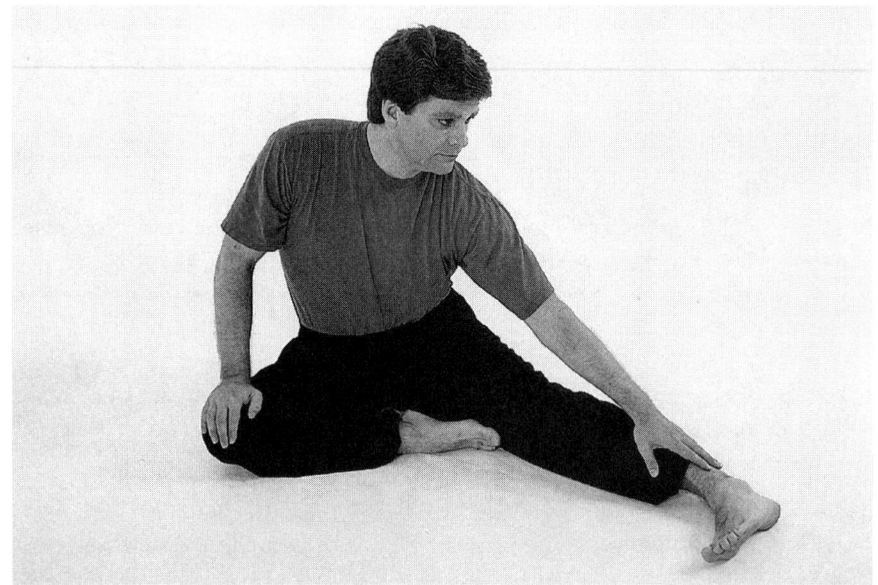

Photo 4.7
Side-Kick Stretch
(first movement)

Second Movement

1. Bend your body forward, with both hands extended in front, and slide your hands forward so your head touches the floor.

2. Rest your upper body on top of your bent right leg.

Photo 4.8
Side-Kick Stretch
(second movement)

Third Movement

1. Slowly raise your upper body to a sitting position, lifting your arms over your head.
2. Slowly bend at your waist as you lower your arms toward your left leg.
3. Hold your left ankle or leg with your left hand and keep your right arm over your head.
4. Breathe deeply, and hold this position for 5 seconds.
5. Bring your arms in front of you, and then repeat the entire series of movements.
6. Repeat the stretch with your right leg out to the side and your left leg bent.

Photo 4.9
Side-Kick Stretch (third movement)

9. Piriformis Stretch

The piriformis stretch isolates a huge, deep muscle group that lies under the gluteal muscles of the buttocks. This important muscle group also lies over the sciatic nerve, which starts at the spine and runs the length of the leg down toward the foot. Anyone who has had sciatic pain knows that it shoots down the legs. This is one of the most effective stretches for relieving sciatic pain. It is especially useful for athletes involved in running, jumping, or kicking movements. The piriformis stretch must be done with control and patience.

1. Kneel on the floor, supporting your upper-body weight with your arms in front of your leg.

2. Slowly move your left leg in front of you, keeping the knee bent, and stretch your straight right leg out behind you (with the bottom of the foot pointing toward the ceiling).

3. Using your hands, position yourself over the center of your left leg. For those who are not flexible yet, this position provides a strong stretch.

Photo 4.10
Piriformis Stretch

4. Hold your position for 10 to 20 seconds, and then repeat the stretch with your right leg in front and your left leg behind.

For a Challenge

In step 3, lean over the front leg, placing your forearms on the floor, and attempt to touch your head to the floor.

Key Points to Remember

- Even if you are not able to perform the more advanced movement, this stretch builds strength in the arms when you are holding the initial position.
- Control is important in this stretch, and it will enhance your coordination and balance.

10. Standing Quad Pose

This is another active stretch, with two parts. If you do this exercise daily, you will notice an improvement in coordination and balance in your everyday activities and your chosen sports. For this and the next exercise (toes over head), the sets and reps are slightly different. Everyone should do 5 repetitions, holding each position for 5 seconds. If you are a beginner—do 2 sets; intermediate—do 4 sets; and advanced—do 5 sets.

First Movement

1. Stand with your feet shoulder-width apart.
2. Bend your left knee, grab your left ankle, and pull your left foot toward your buttocks.
3. Simultaneously raise your right arm above your head, with the fingers pointing toward the ceiling. (For more of a stretch, pull your foot up higher toward your waistline.)
4. With control, rise onto the ball of your right foot (a calf-raise motion).
5. Hold for 5 seconds, and slowly come out of the calf raise.

Photo 4.11
Standing Quad Pose

Second Movement

1. Release your left foot and slowly bring your knee up toward your chest.

2. Hold your knee close to your chest with both hands for 5 seconds.

3. Repeat the entire sequence on the opposite leg.

Key Points to Remember

- If your calves become fatigued before you complete the sets, remain flat-footed.

- Balance and control are key to this movement.
- As you develop more flexibility and balance, the exercise will become easier.

11. Toes over Head

This exercise provides a deep stretch in your lower back and legs and effectively strengthens the abdominal muscles. If you are unable to move your legs past your head because you lack flexibility or strength in your lower back, placing your hands behind your lower back will help you complete the exercise. If you feel a strain in the neck region, you can also place a chair behind you (as shown in Photo 4.12) and hold onto the chair legs with your hands, or place your hands on your lower-back region. When you bring your feet up, you can rest them on the chair.

1. Start by lying on your back, with your arms resting by your sides and with your legs stretched out and relaxed. Keep your lower back flat on the floor.
2. Raise both feet toward the ceiling, lifting your buttocks and lower back off the floor, and moving your feet toward your head.
3. Slowly lower your feet to the ground past your head.

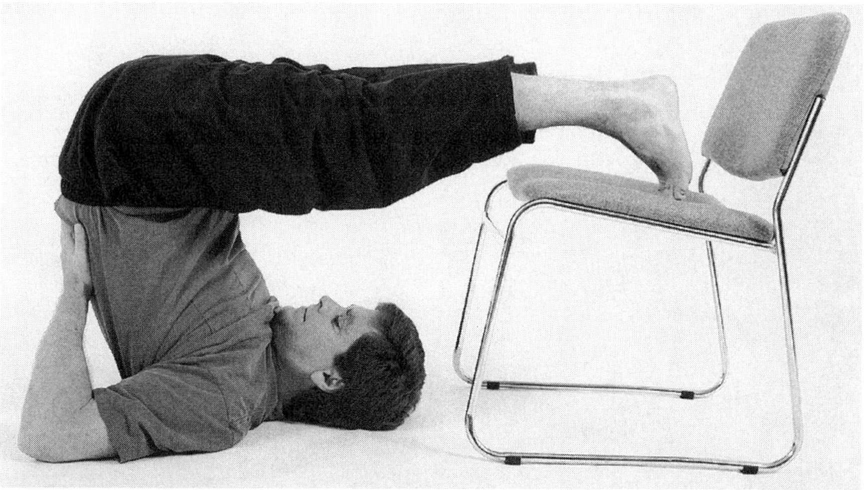

Photo 4.12
Toes over Head

4. Hold this position for 5 seconds, concentrating on deep breathing and relaxing your muscles.

5. Slowly return your legs to the starting position, and repeat the movement.

12. Standing Back Stretch

This last stretch of the BackSmart Daily Dozen series works best with a chair or a bench to rest your leg on. It's a convenient way to stretch your lower back in any location. Beginners should complete 2 sets of 5 repetitions. Those at intermediate and advanced levels should complete 5 sets of 10 repetitions.

1. Stand to the side of the chair and place your left foot on the seat.

2. Slowly bend your upper body forward, dropping your hands toward your right foot.

3. Complete a series of repetitions with your left leg on the chair, and then repeat with the right leg on the chair.

Photo 4.13
Standing Back Stretch

Key Points to Remember

- You will be aware of a slight twist in your hips toward your right side.
- Don't bounce as you perform this exercise; slowly and smoothly allow your body to go as far as it can naturally.

THE BENEFITS OF WARMING UP WITH THE BACKSMART DAILY DOZEN

Brandon, a strong, 27-year-old athlete, excelled at any sport he chose, but he kept getting injured. He would typically do a few warm-up stretches consisting of some toe touches and arm circles before jumping into a game of ball. After a few minutes of running around, he would notice his muscles tightening up, but he would play through it like the true "jock" that he was. After several weekend-warrior events, he noticed that the stiffness and pain from his workouts were not going away.

When he came into my office, I could tell from the way he walked that his hamstrings were too tight; his shoulders were rounded forward, and he held his head too far forward. I began pointing these findings out to him and told him he needed to treat his warm-up time like a professional athlete if he wanted to continue to do sports without suffering from recurring injuries. He invested time in learning the BackSmart Daily Dozen and not only played better at his sports but also excelled at them without the usual aches and pains he had before. His friends were amazed at his newfound flexibility, and he remained in the game longer.

WALL STRETCHES

I developed these wall stretches when I could not sit on the floor to do stretches without experiencing back pain. They are highly effective exercises that will build flexibility and muscular endurance without compressing your spine. I initially instruct all of my patients, including those with disk problems, to regularly perform these stretches before they begin the BackSmart Daily Dozen floor stretches. If you are very inflexible and find that just having your legs out in front of you is uncomfortable, then begin with wall stretches. Performing these stretches will reduce the likelihood of injury and increase power and flexibility in the legs, hips, and arms. The wall stretches can be done in 10 minutes if you are pressed for time.

Several of the stretches in this section can be performed in the smallest of spaces, including in the shower. Shower stretches can be done when you experience stiffness and soreness upon waking up, when your body is simply refusing to get going properly! The shower stretches are the same as the wall stretches done while you're standing, except you perform them in the shower with the hot water on your body to relax the area you are stretching, and include the following:

- Calf and Achilles tendon stretches
- Quadriceps stretch
- Hip stretch
- Neck stretch
- Shoulder and trapezius stretch
- Chest stretch

The wall stretches can be done at any level of flexibility, and people at all levels should complete each stretch as follows: 2 to 4 total sets of 10 to 12 repetitions, holding each stretch for 30 seconds to a minute.

Calf and Achilles Tendon Stretches

This calf stretch easily increases the flexibility in your calf muscles, and the Achilles stretch further reduces the likelihood of an injury to the Achilles tendon, located right behind your ankle.

Calf Stretch

1. Stand facing a wall, two to three feet away from it.

2. Step forward with your right leg and place your hands on the wall at about shoulder height, with your back and left leg straight. (For a more advanced stretch: keep your feet in the same position and lean on your elbows.)

3. Hold this position for 30 seconds to a minute; release and repeat.

4. After completing the reps, repeat the exercise with your left leg forward.

Photo 4.14
Calf Stretch

Achilles Tendon Stretch

1. Stand facing the wall with your feet a few inches apart and about six inches from the wall. Slide your right foot forward so your toes are against the wall and resting higher than your heel.

2. Keep your heel on the floor and make sure your leg is straight. (You should feel a deep stretch throughout your lower-calf region and into your ankle.)

3. Hold for 30 seconds to a minute, and repeat with your other leg.

Photo 4.15
Achilles Tendon Stretch

Quadriceps Stretch

This stretch, which uses gravity to enhance the range of motion, is a great alternative to stretch out the front of your thighs.

1. Stand facing the wall, about two inches away from it.

2. Grab your right foot with your right hand and raise your leg so that your heel hits your buttocks.

Photo 4.16
Quadriceps Stretch

3. Lean forward and rest your right thigh against the wall.

4. Hold the position for 30 seconds to a minute, return to the starting position, and repeat.

5. Complete the reps and then switch to the left leg.

Photo 4.17
Hip Stretch

Hip Stretch

This next stretch is great for the commonly ignored muscles on the side of your hip, which runners frequently injure.

1. Stand with your left arm toward the wall, about two feet away from it, with your feet shoulder-width apart.

2. Place your left leg behind your right leg, lean into the wall, and support yourself with your left arm.

3. Hold this stretch for 30 seconds to a minute.

4. After completing the set of reps, repeat with your right arm on the wall, stretching the opposite hip.

Photo 4.18
Hamstring Stretch

Hamstring Stretch

This movement allows you to stretch the hamstrings, which are commonly tight, without straining your back.

1. Lie on your back on the floor, perpendicular to the wall. Move as close as possible to the wall and attempt to push your buttocks against it.

2. With your legs straight above you resting against the wall, turn your feet outward. (If your hamstrings are tight, you will feel this stretch immediately.)

3. Hold this position each time for 30 seconds to a minute.

4. For a variation, keep your feet together or turn them inward while stretching.

Adductor Stretch

This movement achieves the same stretch as the "splits," but without the strain. When you perform an adductor stretch while lying on the floor, balance is not an issue and gravity assists in bringing your legs down toward the floor.

1. Assume the hamstring position from the previous exercise—against the wall with your legs up.

2. Separate your legs as much as possible.

3. After reaching your maximum range of motion, place your hands on the inside of your thighs.

4. Using active resistance to enhance your flexibility, push up with your legs while pushing down with your hands.

5. Provide resistance for 6 seconds, stop, return to the starting position, and repeat.

Photo 4.19
Adductor Stretch

Back Stretch

If you have limited time to exercise, this one position can be done easily throughout the day to stretch all the muscles that run along your spine, to keep you supple.

1. Stand a few feet out from the wall with your back against it, knees bent (so that your thighs are parallel to the floor), and feet shoulder-width apart.

2. Place your arms up against the wall, bent at the elbows (as if you are holding a crossing-guard sign).

Photo 4.20
Back Stretch

3. With your hands in an open position, keep your wrists, head, and entire back flat against the wall and tuck your chin slightly downward.

4. Breathe deeply and hold for 1 minute, return to the starting position, and repeat.

Neck Stretch

This is a great movement for stretching the lower-neck and upper-back muscles safely and effectively.

1. Stand facing the wall about two feet away, with your feet about six inches apart.

Photo 4.21
Neck Stretch

2. Lean forward and place your hands on the wall, about two feet above your head.

3. Slowly lower your head and feel the stretch.

4. Hold the position for 30 seconds to a minute and repeat.

Shoulder and Trapezius Stretch

This is a great stretch for relieving soreness in the commonly ignored muscles of the lower neck.

1. Assume the same neck position from the previous exercise.

2. Take one step forward with your right leg and rest your elbows against the wall, with your head down as you look toward your feet. (Your hands should be about 10 inches apart.)

Photo 4.22
Shoulder and Trapezius Stretch

3. Slowly turn your hands out until your palms are facing each other, which will increase the stretch in the shoulder area.

4. Hold this position for 30 seconds to a minute, return to the starting position, and repeat.

Chest Stretch

This last wall stretch enhances the flexibility of your chest area, so you will improve your range of motion for throwing and racket sports.

1. Stand facing a corner, about two feet away. Place each arm on a wall above shoulder level and lean forward into the corner. Place one leg forward and the opposite leg back for a strong stance.

Photo 4.23
Chest Stretch

2. Hold the stretch for 30 seconds to a minute.

3. Push yourself away from the corner, return to the starting position, and repeat.

HOW WALL STRETCHES CAN HELP DURING LONG HOURS AT A DESK JOB

Kathy, a 27-year-old computer tech, traveled a lot. In addition to spending long hours traveling, Kathy would sit in front of her computer doing work, hunched over for hours on end. She started to develop tension headaches and back and neck stiffness that became progressively worse through the week. By the weekend, all Kathy wanted to do was lie down, because that was the most comfortable position for her.

This wasn't the first time I had seen such a person suffering from our modern-day lifestyle, nor was it going to be the last. Since Kathy was restricted to her schedule and couldn't steal time away to exercise, the wall stretches were ideal for her condition. She spent most of her time pulling her shoulders and neck forward in front of the computer, and the wall stretches would counterbalance her poor posture position.

After only a few weeks, Kathy reported that she suffered fewer tension headaches and that she used the stretches to prevent the pain pattern from starting when she put in long hours in front of the computer. She is working on changing the way she sits at the computer and makes time to be away from it to help reduce her aches and pains.

GETTING A LEG UP: ADVANCED STRETCHING

Many athletes, from all walks of life, have come into my center after being referred by another athlete who had suffered injury. These athletes had felt like "hanging it up" because of their injuries, until they trained with me using the BackSmart plan. One eye-opener for these athletes, and for people in general who want to stay in shape, is that they spend very little time in developing their flexibility routine. They think that once they can touch their toes or do the splits, there is no more to learn. A common mistake that many competitive athletes, who usually have more flexibility than most people, still make is in not connecting the mind to the stretching process. Because they have been doing the stretches for many years, the movements have become second nature to them.

After teaching the proper positions and breathing techniques, as explained at the beginning of this chapter, I give people with good flexibility the four stretches in this section. Most athletes notice a deeper stretch feeling in the muscles from doing these movements. And just as they have found themselves running faster and suffering from fewer aches and pains, you, too, can experience the benefits from doing these advanced stretches. Don't be fooled by the simplistic nature of these stretches. If you focus on your breathing, you can achieve your goals. The following stretches can be done at various levels of flexibility. As you progress, the movements will remain the same, but the height of the equipment you use will change.

The common household ladder, which usually collects dust out in the garage until it is needed for changing a lightbulb, is perfect for these stretches. You can use it at any flexibility level by starting on a lower rung and working your way up. If a ladder is not available, stairs can also be used to increase progress. When you increase the elevation of your leg, you will feel a tremendous stretch in your hamstrings, calves, and buttocks. As your flexibility and balance improve, you will be able to raise your leg higher.

I have been doing these stretches since I was a child training in martial arts. These moves may even make you feel as if you are Jackie Chan, the movie star. They are effective for stretching your legs and lower back when minimum space is available. For these ladder stretches, people at all levels should complete each stretch as follows: 2 sets of 10 to 20 repetitions, holding each stretch for 5 seconds.

Front Leg Raise

Standing on one leg will help improve your sense of balance and coordination. In addition, you will increase your flexibility and feel the entire muscle group being stretched. If you need help keeping your balance, support yourself by holding onto a chair or leaning against a wall.

1. Raise your right leg and place your foot on the equipment, keeping your upper body straight. Keep your leg straight and place it at the height of your waist.

Photo 4.24
Front Leg Raise

2. Relax at the waist, and reach out over your toes with your hands.

3. Hold for 5 seconds, return to starting position, and repeat.

4. After completing a set, repeat with your other leg.

Bent-Knee Stretch

This stretch is similar to the standing back stretch that concludes the BackSmart Daily Dozen. By raising your leg higher, you will feel a deeper stretch in the buttocks and back muscles.

1. Stand to the side of the equipment and place your right foot on a rung so that your foot is higher than your left knee.

2. Slowly bend your upper body forward, dropping your hands toward your left foot. (You will be aware of a slight twist in your hips toward your

Photo 4.25
Bent-Knee Stretch

left side. Don't bounce as you perform this exercise; slowly and smoothly allow your body to go as far as it can naturally.)

3. Hold for 5 seconds, return to the starting position, and repeat.

4. Complete a set of repetitions, and then repeat with your other foot on the equipment.

Standing Side-Kick Stretch

This next stretch works a hard-to-reach region—behind your leg and the inner thigh.

1. Stand with your right side toward the equipment and place your right foot on a rung. Keep your leg straight and place your leg as high as your waist or higher.

Photo 4.26
Standing Side-Kick Stretch

2. Turn your leg so the foot lies sideways (with the outside of your foot pointing up).

3. Standing tall, reach with both arms toward your outstretched leg.

4. Hold for 5 seconds, return to starting position, and repeat.

5. Complete a set; then repeat with your other leg on the equipment.

Standing Bent-Leg Twist

With this last ladder stretch, you will feel a deep stretch in your hips and gluteal muscles as well as the lower-back muscles.

1. Stand to the side of the equipment, and place your right foot on a rung at least knee-high and preferably higher (to feel the stretch effectively).

Photo 4.27
Standing Bent-Leg Twist

2. Turn your upper body to the right, place your left elbow against your right leg, and lean forward slightly. Extend your right arm out to the side, away from your body.

3. After completing a set, repeat with your other leg.

INCORPORATING THE LADDER STRETCHES INTO YOUR REGULAR ROUTINE

Scott, a 51-year-old electrician, came to me with a neck injury he had sustained while playing football with his kids. He said he had remained fairly active with his kids, but sometimes after work, he felt too stiff to play with them, and he thought that was probably why he had injured himself. I showed him how to perform the advanced stretches right away, which I normally don't do, but since he was up and down on a ladder all day, it was the perfect fit.

He said the guys ribbed him a little in the beginning when they saw him use his ladder in ways they never thought possible, but over time some of his coworkers gave the stretches a try. He said that after a few weeks, he felt less tight, and by stretching throughout the day, he stayed limber and could play with his kids again after work without sustaining any injuries due to muscle tightness.

Now that you have stretched out your body in this chapter, you are ready to work on your abdominal muscles. You will continue moving your body as a unit, using your limbs in a rhythmic pattern while focusing on your center.

CHAPTER 5

STRENGTHEN YOUR ABDOMINAL MUSCLES FOR A STRONGER BACK

I'll say it now: this is one muscle group that you can do every day and then some—similar to our calves, the muscles in our legs, which we use every day. We do a lot of walking, running, stepping, and so forth, resulting in fibers of high density. Similarly, our abs hold the spine upright and keep our intestines in, for the most part. They help us bend, turn, and twist repeatedly during all of our waking and sleeping hours.

BACKSMART PILATES

If you haven't been caught up in the Pilates craze, you probably have either tried or at least heard of this exercise regimen. While many people who do not suffer from back pain can perform the traditional Pilates movements without injuries, the majority of people do not have the core strength to do them injury-free, and it is not widely known that some of the movements can cause undue stress to the lower back. With this in mind, I have changed leg positions and the length of some movements to keep the exercises safe and effective for those who have suffered from back and neck pain. This modified version of Pilates allows exercisers to work out without causing harm to the vulnerable upper and lower vertebrae.

Benefits of BackSmart Pilates

In Pilates classes, instructors will tell you to "use your core" when executing movements. These exercises work the core muscles—the lower abdominals, spinal erectors, and hip flexors—with efficiency, while also building muscular endurance in the midsection and legs in a short period. Pilates exercises strengthen the muscles without bulking you up, toning and shaping the body to give it a lean, athletic look. These exercises can help you to better control your muscles and enhance your body awareness. Learning to work multiple muscle groups in an integrated way, using proper breathing and balance techniques, also improves your posture as it helps you to control your glutes and hip muscles, giving you that shapely, defined athletic look while preventing back pain.

MODIFYING PILATES FOR REDUCED STRESS ON THE BACK

Julie was a 26-year-old ice-skating instructor. When she competed, she used to train for up to five or six hours a day. Now she was still on the ice, but she didn't burn the number of calories she did when she was competing. She had tried the health club but didn't find it to be the right atmosphere for her. Being competitive, she liked to challenge herself, and either the classes she took were too easy for her or she would try too hard and strain her back.

Julie said she tried Pilates, but she felt her lower back being strained during the more advanced movements. I introduced her to the BackSmart modified Pilates workout. She was able to do the exercises at home before she went to the rink. She said she found the exercises challenging, and they were effective in strengthening her midsection.

Key Points to Remember When Doing BackSmart Pilates

- Breathing deeply and relaxing during the movements increases the benefits of the activity.

- Pilates is a functional workout that challenges the body to work collectively as a whole, firing up the muscles in a sequential pattern.

- Stay relaxed while tensing your midsection.
- Do not hold your breath during the strengthening phase of the movement.
- Do not sacrifice form for strength.
- Do these movements on a mat or carpeted area.

BACKSMART PILATES WORKOUT

You'll find that most of the exercises in this series have a "BackSmart Alternative" that will put less strain on the back. I point out alternate positions within the step sequence or suggest alternate movements at the end of the exercise. Many times, I also include a more advanced movement, "For a Challenge," at the end of the exercise, for those who already have strong abdominal muscles and want to go further. The amount of time it takes you to complete the circuit of exercises listed here will depend on the shape you are in to begin with. For example, if you have never done these types of movements or are new to exercising in general, it will take you approximately 15 to 25 minutes. As endurance and strength build, you'll be able to complete the exercises more times without stopping, and the whole sequence can take around 10 to 15 minutes.

If you've taken traditional Pilates classes, you'll probably find that I suggest more repetitions for each of the exercises than what you experienced in class. The reason behind this is that I have found that with my patients who are either just starting out in an exercise routine or suffering from back pain, the body requires more time to incorporate the proper muscle groups, learn the patterns, and get into a groove in order to feel the appropriate muscles working. Thus, in my BackSmart Pilates program, I have incorporated more repetitions in order to achieve this goal.

When learning these BackSmart Pilates movements (with the exception of the first one—hundreds), people at all levels should complete each exercise as follows: 2 to 3 sets of 10 to 20 repetitions.

Hundreds

This first exercise is used as a warm-up and breathing exercise that emphasizes the abdominal muscles, which will improve posture and support the lower back.

1. Start by lying on your back, with your arms by your sides and your hands flat on the floor. Point your feet and lengthen your spine.

2. Lift your head toward your chest, and lift your legs 90 degrees, maintaining a flat lower back.

BackSmart Alternative

Keep your knees bent, instead of straight, to reduce the stress on the lower back.

---

3. With small, controlled movements, use a pumping action to lift and lower your straight arms (raise them about three inches).

4. Inhale as you move your arms up and down for 5 seconds, and then exhale as you move your arms up and down for the next 5 seconds.

5. Continue inhaling and exhaling rhythmically until you've reached 100 repetitions. (Your abdominal muscles should start to burn after 50 or 60 repetitions.) This is the only exception to the rule for the number of

Photo 5.1
Hundreds

repetitions. You will complete 100 reps per set rather than 10 to 20 repetitions.

For a Challenge

For a more advanced movement, lower your legs to 45 degrees to activate more lower-abdominal muscle groups.

Corkscrew

The corkscrew emphasizes abdominals, hip flexors and extensors, and spinal erectors in the lower-back region, which will help you achieve greater coordination and improved motion. Make sure to hold in your abdominal muscles and to use your hip and leg muscles for this exercise.

1. Lie flat on your back with your arms by your sides.

2. Exhale as you slowly raise your legs 90 degrees.

Photo 5.2
Corkscrew

BackSmart Alternative

Keep your legs slightly bent during the exercise to prevent back strain.

3. Inhale as you move your legs and hips clockwise as one unit, and exhale as you complete each circle.

4. Complete 10 repetitions clockwise, and then repeat the exercise moving your legs and hips counterclockwise, for 1 full set.

5. Start with small circles to keep control of the movement. As you develop more strength and flexibility, you can do larger circles.

For a Challenge

This advanced movement will work more of the lower-back and lower-abdominal area:

1. Bring your legs over your head, letting your toes touch the floor behind you.

2. Slowly raise your feet, rotate them around to the beginning position, and repeat.

Scissors

This is a good exercise for control and balance because of its emphasis on lower-body movement and concentration. You'll be engaging the hip flexors and extensors, the lower-abdominal region, and the lower-back region for increased flexibility and lower-abdominal strength as well as improved coordination and range of motion.

1. Lie flat on the floor with your arms by your sides.

2. Exhale as you slowly lift your legs. Simultaneously place your hands, palms up, behind the small of your back, resting your elbows on the floor for support.

Photo 5.3
Scissors

3. Point your toes toward the ceiling, stretching your legs as far as you can. (Keep your feet directly above your face as you stretch upward.)

4. Begin a slow and controlled scissors motion with your legs—one leg moving toward your face while the other leg is moving toward the floor. Rhythmically inhale and exhale as you alternate your legs during the movement.

BackSmart Alternative

1. If you have lower-back pain, instead of positioning your feet above your face, raise your legs only about 45 degrees.

2. Stretch your arms out in front and reach toward your feet, with your head raised.

3. Move your legs in the scissors motion while maintaining your arm position.

Double Leg Stretch

As with the previous exercises, the double leg stretch emphasizes abdominals, spinal erectors, and hip flexors, but it also provides a beneficial lower-back stretch while simultaneously strengthening the abdominal muscles. Coordinating your breathing with your movements is important during this exercise.

1. Begin by lying on your back.

2. Bend your knees, grab them, and draw them toward your chest.

3. At the same time, exhale as you raise your chin toward your chest, while contracting your abdominal muscles.

4. Inhale and straighten your legs, raising them 45 degrees as you bring your arms over your head.

5. Circle your arms out to the sides and toward the center, pull your knees in, and repeat the movement. (Make sure your lower back remains flat.)

Photos 5.4, 5.5 Double Leg Stretch

BackSmart Alternative

Performing this modification will reduce stress to the lower-back region and is an option for people who are less flexible:

1. Keep one leg stationary, with the knee bent and the foot flat on the floor.

2. Perform the movement as described, but with just one leg.

Seal

This movement (also called "rolling like a ball"), which relaxes your back muscles and improves your spine's flexibility, emphasizes lower-back spinal erectors and abdominals.

1. Sit up tall, with your feet flat on the floor and knees bent.

2. Reach forward and grab your ankles. (Continue holding your ankles throughout the sequence.)

3. Inhale as you pull your legs toward your chest, and rock backward until your back touches the floor.

Photos 5.6, 5.7 Seal

4. Exhale and curl upward, returning to a seated, balance position (similar to the beginning position, but with your feet off the floor).

5. Inhale as you rock backward, and repeat the sequence.

For a Challenge

To further increase balance, strength, and coordination:

1. After curling upward, stay in this seated, balance position for 2 seconds before rocking backward.

2. Concentrate on the balance position.

Teaser

This next exercise builds strong abdominals and improves balance, by emphasizing the abdominals, spinal erectors, and hip flexors.

1. Sit up tall, with your knees bent, feet flat, and hands resting on the floor.

2. Inhale as you extend your legs forward and up. (The strength of your stomach muscles and your flexibility will determine how high you will be able to raise your legs, but they will remain in a raised position throughout the sequence.)

Photos 5.8, 5.9 Teaser

3. Maintain your balance as you raise your arms toward your feet.

4. Exhale and slowly lower yourself backward, until your back is flat on the floor.

5. Slowly curl back up to the sitting position, and repeat.

BackSmart Alternative

Beginners and anyone wanting less stress on the back can perform the exercise as described, but with only one leg extended. As strength increases, both legs can be extended.

Hip Circles

The emphasis on leg control in this movement enhances balance and coordination, targeting the lower abdominals and hip flexors.

1. Sit up tall, with your hands on the floor behind your back for support.

2. Contract your abdominal muscles as you raise your legs as high as you can. (Keep your legs together, with a slight bend at the knees and your toes pointed.)

Photo 5.10
Hip Circles

3. Move your legs clockwise in a large circular pattern. (Your feet will come close to the floor, but do not let them touch the floor.)

4. Complete 10 circles, exhaling and inhaling with every full circle, and then repeat the exercise in the opposite direction.

BackSmart Alternative

If you have less flexibility or want less stress on your back, perform the exercise as described, but with more bending at the knees until strength and flexibility develop.

Side Leg Lifts

As in hip circles, the emphasis on leg control in this movement enhances balance and coordination and targets the muscles in the inner and outer thighs and hips.

1. Lie on your right side and maintain a straight back while contracting your abdominal muscles. Keep your legs stretched out, with your head either resting on your arm or supported by your right hand. Place your left hand on the floor near your stomach.

2. Lift both legs about two feet from the floor.

3. Inhale and slowly lower your right leg, keeping the left leg up. (Your legs should not be touching the floor at any point during this sequence.)

4. Exhale as you lift your right leg until it is touching the left leg.

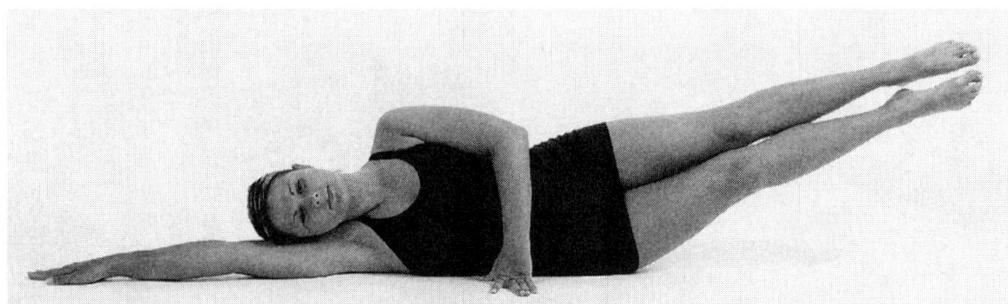

Photo 5.11
Side Leg Lifts

5. Complete 10 to 12 more repetitions of lowering and raising your right leg, change sides, and repeat.

Single Straight Leg

This exercise provides a strong hamstring, gluteal, and abdominal stretch, which results in more flexible legs—thus reducing the stress on the lower back.

1. Lie flat on your back with your arms by your sides.

2. Keep your right leg straight and raise it toward the ceiling.

3. Exhale as you curl your upper body up, reach with both hands, and grab your calf area.

4. Hold for 2 seconds, and then inhale as you release your calf and lower your upper body back to starting position.

5. Switch legs, and repeat the movement.

Photo 5.12
Single Straight Leg

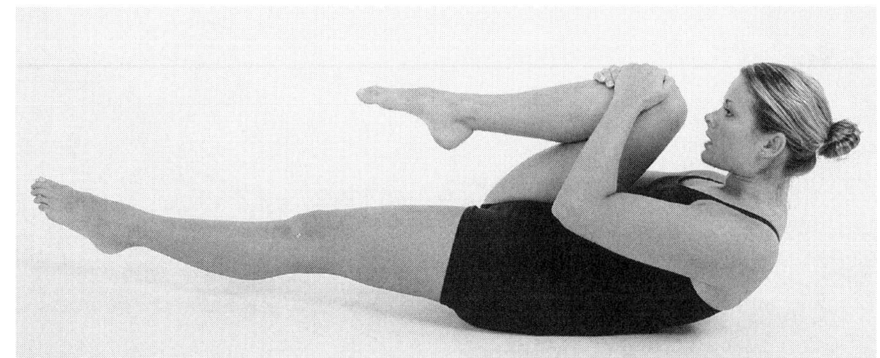

Photo 5.13
Single Straight Leg
(bent-knee alternative)

BackSmart Alternative

If you are less flexible, you can do this exercise with a bent leg until your strength and flexibility are developed. As you curl up, bend your knee and draw in the leg. (You can grab either your calf or your knee for this modified movement.)

Jackknife

This last exercise will also work toward preventing back injuries as it increases flexibility in the lower back by strengthening the abdominal muscles. Through stabilizing your leg movement here, you will also develop strength and control.

1. Lie on your back, with your legs straight out in front and arms by your sides.

2. Exhale and slowly raise your legs, reaching for 90 degrees.

3. Lift your hips until you are resting on your shoulders and arms. Hold this position for 1 or 2 seconds.

4. Slowly roll down and lower your legs while inhaling.

5. Repeat the entire sequence.

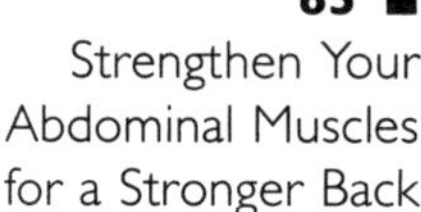

Photo 5.14
Jackknife

INCORPORATING BACKSMART PILATES INTO YOUR ROUTINE FOR POSITIVE RESULTS

Steve was a 57-year-old lawyer who had gained some weight around his midsection even though he played squash two times a week instead of eating lunch. He complained that he wasn't moving the way he wanted and his spare tire was getting in his way. He didn't feel he could do a workout at the gym after he played squash because the activity took too much out of him, and he didn't have time to get to the gym on other days.

The modified Pilates were perfect for Steve; he could do the exercises at home as well as at his office—when he closed his door, no one was the wiser. After just a few months, people began commenting on Steve's new look. He said he was losing weight and felt his game had improved since he started the BackSmart program.

As you can see from performing these modified movements, you no longer will suffer from back or neck strain when doing the Pilates exercises. By doing the modified exercises in this manner and sequence, you will work your midsection effectively while stretching out your hamstrings and hip flexors and enhancing your muscular endurance.

The bonus to doing these functional movements is that you will not bulk up, but rather tone and shape your body, giving you that lean, athletic look; your posture will improve, and you will have better coordination and balance. In the next part of the chapter, you will learn how to work your entire midsection.

BOOT CAMP FOR TIGHTER, STRONGER ABDOMINALS

There can never be too many days to work your stomach into a flat, firm body part. However, the key is the sequence of different exercises performed on different days. Working the stomach muscles from different angles and intensity levels throughout the week will help assure a strong and supportive midsection, which is important for spinal control and lifting motions.

The center of the body—the width of your girth—is usually a visual indicator of what kind of shape you are in. Your midsection is a sign of your fitness level and ability to maintain your ideal body weight. The following discussion explains how to maximize the benefits as well as avoid potentially serious mistakes commonly made when exercising these muscle groups. For example, doing only crunches for endless numbers of repetitions and not employing a greater range of motion during the exercise will result in tight, inflexible muscles, as well as poor posture.

Now that you have learned the various BackSmart Pilates movements for building a stronger core, it's time to move on to the many different ab routines that I've provided here to keep you working this area so that it is even stronger. With this program, you can forget about boredom because it won't happen. Make it as easy as you want or harder on those days when you want to push yourself, with more repetitions and high-volume workouts. So, put away those ab toys that promise you flatter abs in minutes, and get ready to have a challenging and fun workout.

Abdominal Position

I am consistently reminded that visually pleasing abdominals are not necessarily strong. Many patients have come to me over the years telling me they work their stomach muscles hard every day—"I do at least a hundred crunches every day!" Then I ask them to try my way, not using momentum or simply lifting their heads off the floor as if they are bobbing for apples.

The abdominal position requires lying on your back with the knees bent and feet up, just so you see the top of your toes. In this way, your body mechanics can emphasize the muscles being worked with a minimum amount of stress to the spinal region and the hip flexor muscles that pull on the spine.

Breathing

When doing these exercises, concentrate on holding in and squeezing your abdominal muscles rather than breathing. I see many people performing their

WHY SLOW AND CONTROLLED ABDOMINAL WORK IS MORE EFFECTIVE

Michael was a 47-year-old professor who had been an active tennis player and golfer until two years ago, when he pulled his back. He explained: "I would play tennis in the winter and golf in the summer up to that point. But I had to give up tennis because I felt too much pain in my back. I went to every specialist in town and tried working with a trainer, all to no avail. Golf still hurts too, but not as much."

After evaluating Michael, I watched him swing the tennis racket and golf club and also observed how he performed some of the exercises he did at the gym. I noticed that he would do very fast repetitions during his abdominal workout.

I showed him the BackSmart abdominal routine, and he could finish only half of the repetitions because he felt his abdominals working so effectively. However, after about a month of training the BackSmart way, not only was Michael stronger and more fit, but also he began playing tennis again.

abdominal exercises as if they were doing aerobics, breathing out forcefully, trying to time it with the movement, which is almost impossible.

Near the end of your sets, when you begin to fatigue and your muscles are starving for more oxygen, you will breathe faster naturally. However, make sure you are not holding your breath, as that's even worse. It's like trying to burst a balloon filled with air.

ABDOMINAL EXERCISES FOR THE WEEK

The recommended order in which to do the abdominal exercises is as a giant super set—going through 1 set of each exercise in sequence and then resting. Then you repeat the order for another set. To give you a practical example, I have provided you with a week's worth of abdominal movements. For beginners, this will be enough of a workout for you to start with over the next four to six weeks. As you become stronger over the weeks, you can change the exercises around, remembering to focus on two areas of your midsection in each workout. Perform 1 set of each exercise before returning to the beginning exercise; then rest and repeat. Intermediate and advanced exercisers can add up to three movements per session to enhance your strength and definition in your midsection.

At the beginning, you will start with upper abdominals, followed by lower abdominals, and then the oblique region, working all angles in a true strong and athletic routine for the abdominal region.

Now it's time to have some fun—and remember that after learning these movements, you can change the days or exercises around to suit your desire. When learning these abdominal movements, all levels should complete each exercise as follows: 2 to 4 sets of 10 to 25 repetitions.

If you have been exercising for more than a year and you can complete a full circuit of movements at 4 sets each, you can move on to the next section of this chapter, where you'll be adding an advanced movement to your program each day to enhance your strength and tone your midsection.

Monday Ab Exercises

For your first day of abdominal exercises, you'll be doing different types of slow and controlled crunches that emphasize primary upper and lower abdominals.

Crunches—Hands on Knees

1. Lie on your back with your knees bent.

2. Without lifting your head, and keeping your knees together, raise your legs (about three feet above the floor) until you see the top of your feet. (Hold that leg position throughout the movement.)

3. Place your hands on your knees and slowly curl up, working your fingers up toward your feet.

4. Hold at the top for 2 seconds before lowering to the starting position; repeat.

Key Points to Remember

- Do not bend your knees toward your chest; keep them at 90 degrees with your hips.
- To isolate your abdominals, contract your abdominal muscles strongly at the top of the movement.
- Execute this movement slowly; a bad habit is to rush through this exercise.

Photo 5.15
Crunch—
Hands on Knees

Reverse Crunches

1. Lie on your back with your knees bent. Keep your arms by your sides throughout the movement.

2. Keeping your knees together, raise your feet (about three feet above the floor) until you see the top of your feet, and hold.

3. Slowly curl your hips off the floor toward your shoulders, and squeeze for 2 seconds at the top.

4. Slowly curl your hips back down to the starting position, and repeat.

Photo 5.16
Reverse Crunch

Tuesday Ab Exercises

For the next day of abdominal exercises, you'll continue to work the primary lower and upper abdominals.

Crunches—Butterfly Position

1. Lie on your back, and keep your feet in contact with the floor throughout this exercise.

2. Slowly bend your legs outward and bring your feet in toward your groin. (Keep the bottom of your feet together throughout the movement.)

3. Place your hands on the back of your head, slowly curl up, and hold at the top of the movement for 2 seconds.

4. Return to the beginning position and repeat.

BackSmart Alternative

If you suffer from neck strains, keep your hands by your ears.

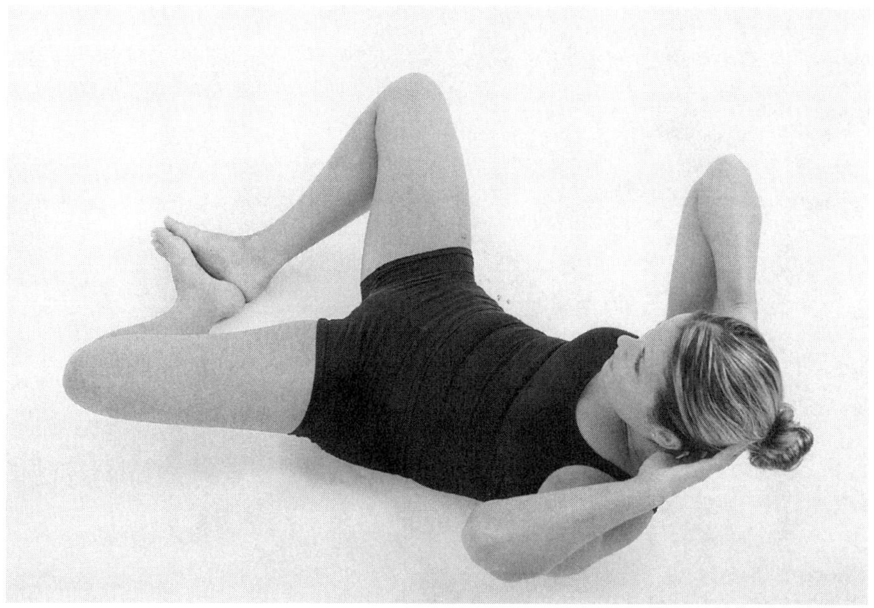

Photo 5.17
Crunch—
Butterfly Position

For a Challenge

If you are at a more advanced level, stretch your arms up straight over your head instead of placing your hands behind your neck.

Hip Raises

1. Lie on your back, with your arms by your sides and your legs raised straight up but with a slight bend in your knees and your feet together and pointing toward the ceiling.

2. Slowly squeezing your stomach muscles, lift your hips off the floor and roll them toward your chest.

3. Pause when your feet are above your head, and hold for 2 seconds.

4. Slowly lower your hips back to the floor until you return to the starting position, and repeat.

Photo 5.18
Hip Raise

Wednesday Ab Exercises

After the first two days of your BackSmart program, you will begin to feel parts of your midsection that you didn't know you had. There may be an unfamiliar soreness on your sides as you work the deep supportive muscle groups that help stabilize your body's center. Do not coast now: keep going through the rest of the week.

Toe-Touch Crunches with a Twist

1. Lie on your back, with your legs raised and feet pointing up, and your arms above your head.
2. Reach up with both arms, and try to touch your right hand to your left foot.
3. Hold for 2 seconds, and then lower slowly to the starting position.

Photo 5.19
Toe-Touch Crunch with a Twist

4. Repeat, with the left hand moving toward your right foot.

5. Repeat the exercise, alternating arms.

V Sit-Ups Against the Wall

1. Lie on your back perpendicular to the wall, with your buttocks touching the wall and your legs up against the wall more than shoulder-width apart. Stretch your arms out over your head.

2. Bring your head forward and reach your arms over and up to touch the wall.

3. Hold for 2 seconds, slowly curl back down, and repeat.

Photo 5.20
V Sit-Up
Against the Wall

Thursday Ab Exercises

For this next day of primary upper- and lower-abdominal exercises, you need a workout bench or chair to do the seated knee-ups.

Seated Knee-Ups

1. Sit on a chair or bench.
2. With your knees together, lean back slightly and lift your feet off the floor. (Place your hands down by your side for support.)
3. Pull your knees toward your chest, and squeeze your abs at the top.
4. Hold for 2 seconds, lower your legs so that you gently touch your feet on the floor, and repeat.

For a Challenge

If you are at a more advanced level, hold a medicine ball between your ankles.

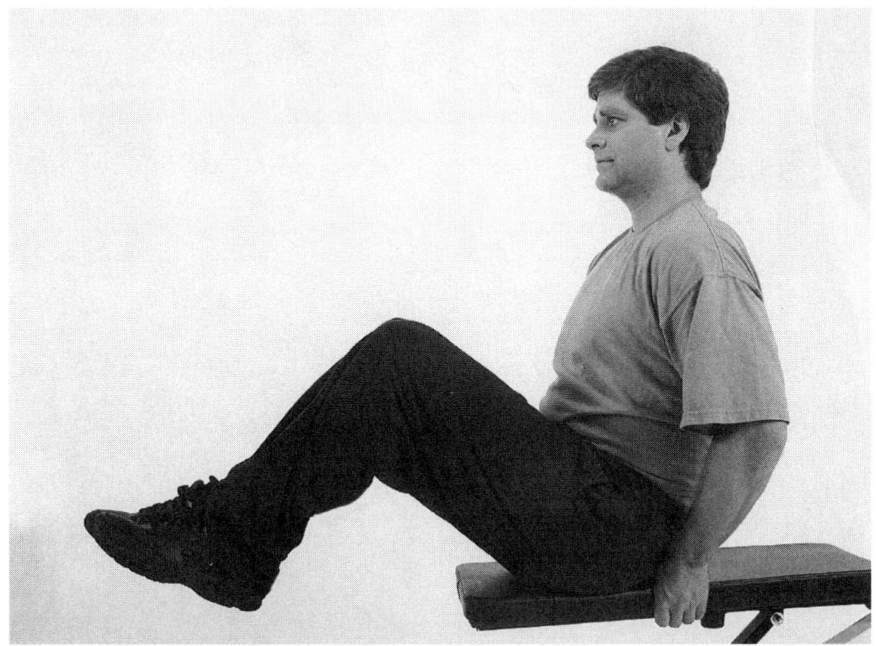

Photo 5.21
Seated Knee-Up

Oblique Side Crunches

1. Lie on your right side, with your knees bent and your torso twisted so that your upper body is facing upward. Place your hands by your ears.

2. Slowly lift your upper body toward your hips and lift your shoulders off the floor.

3. Hold at the top for 2 seconds, lower yourself to the beginning position, and repeat before switching to the opposite side.

For a Challenge

If you are more advanced, place your upper arm above your head and keep it extended straight (not bent) during the entire movement.

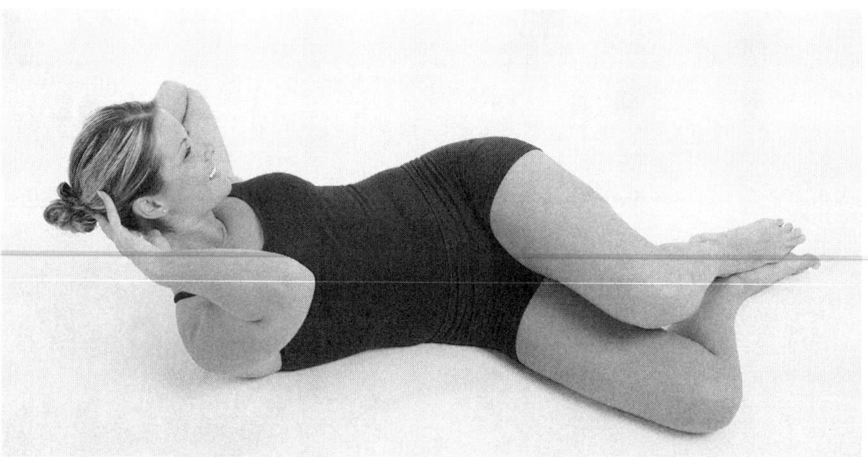

Photo 5.22
Oblique Side Crunch

Friday Ab Exercises

You're almost there; don't give up now. You are on the way to having the strongest midsection possible. For your last day of the week, you'll be doing exercises that emphasize more oblique lower- and upper-abdominal muscles. You can vary the repetitions and sets to intensify your routine or do less on days you feel stiff or sore from a previous workout.

Knees-to-Elbows Side Leg Lifts

1. Lie on your side, resting on your left elbow, with your right hand behind your head and your knees slightly bent.

2. Slowly squeeze in your stomach.

3. Keeping your knees together, raise your legs toward your right elbow.

4. Hold for 2 seconds, and slowly lower your legs.

5. Complete 10 repetitions, and switch to the other side.

Photo 5.23
Knees-to-Elbows Side Leg Lift

Leg Raises on Your Elbows

1. Recline on the floor, resting your upper body on your elbows for support.
2. Raise your legs a few inches, with a slight bend in your knees.
3. Lift your legs up toward your head.
4. Hold for 2 seconds, lower your legs to the floor, and repeat.

BackSmart Alternative

This exercise can be done with bent knees as well:

1. Bring your knees up toward your chest.
2. Push your legs back out, and repeat.

Photo 5.24 Leg Raise on Your Elbows

Congratulations! Saturday and Sunday can be either rest days if you are just starting out or time to repeat the cycle, starting with Tuesday's workout. Once you get used to the soreness in the abdominal region, you can gauge your intensity for the next day's workout. You may feel a slight soreness in the lower-back region if you have never tried working your lower abdominals before, but you should not feel any pain in the lower back.

VARYING YOUR ABDOMINAL ROUTINE

Sean was a 51-year-old karate enthusiast who had trained for more than three decades, winding up with many broken bones, bumps, and bruises along the way, he told me. But his back had started to give him problems over the past five years, to the extent that he would have to take off a week or two at a time. He worked out consistently seven days a week, except when his back problems were flaring up. Even then, he did weights and cardio every other day.

His abdominal workout was the same as it was 30 years ago. Sean never thought to change his routine of sit-ups, push-ups, and chin-ups because he was in much better shape than many people half his age.

I pointed out that he may have been doing more harm than good when it came to his midsection routine by placing a lot of stress on his lower-back region. Since Sean was strong, I gave him the BackSmart advanced abdominal workout. "I was really surprised at how much I felt my 'abs' after trying just one session," he said, "and there was no back pain or soreness. I am hooked." Sean continues to work his midsection every day, but without the pain.

How to Judge When You're Ready to Move to the Next Level

Progressively challenging your stomach region with these exercises will help strengthen the lower-back region by stretching the muscles while you work the abdominals. You know you are ready for the next series of movements if you can perform 4 sets of each movement at the maximum repetitions stated. Or you can test yourself by performing crunches with hands on knees for 60 to 70 repetitions without resting. It is difficult to perform this many crunches all in one set, but doing so is a good indicator that you have gotten stronger and have no back pain when you are doing the movement.

ADVANCED ABDOMINALS

This next group of exercises is designed for the more advanced person looking for a more resistive and challenging workout to build and tone the midsection for a hard and firm abdominal region. For this advanced abdominal workout, you'll need a medicine ball weighing up to 10 pounds. If you don't have one, you can use a soccer ball or basketball.

With each day, I introduce a new challenging exercise, followed by repeats of exercises from the previous section. Warm up with the hundreds exercise, followed by this sequence of exercises, in order to produce a hard and firm midsection and a stronger foundation to help prevent future injuries. When learning these movements, complete each of the exercises as follows: 2 to 4 sets of 10 to 25 repetitions.

Monday Ab Exercises

Monday's abdominal exercises emphasize the primary lower and upper abdominals and require the use of a medicine ball weighing 4 to 5 pounds.

Medicine Ball Crunches in Front

1. Lie on your back, with your knees bent and your legs raised to the point at which you see the top of your feet. Your legs will remain in this position throughout the movement.

2. Hold the ball in your hands close to your chest.

3. Slowly curl up toward your knees.

4. Hold for 2 seconds, lower to the starting position, and repeat.

Follow this movement with the **reverse crunches** and finally the **oblique side crunches** for 4 to 5 sets of 10 to 25 repetitions of each exercise.

Photo 5.25
Medicine Ball Crunch
in Front

Tuesday Ab Exercises

For this next day, you'll be doing some exercises that work both upper and lower abdominals at the same time.

Toe-Touch Crunches with a Medicine Ball Twist

1. Lie on your back, with your legs raised and feet pointing at the ceiling. You will remain in this position throughout.

2. Holding the medicine ball, place your arms above your head.

3. Bring your arms up and over and try to touch your left foot.

4. Hold your arms up for 2 seconds, lower slowly to the starting position, and repeat the movement, reaching toward the other foot.

5. Keep alternating feet as you complete the repetitions.

Photo 5.26
Toe-Touch Crunch with a Medicine Ball Twist

Follow this movement with the **knees-to-elbows side leg lifts**, ending with **toe-touch crunches with a twist**, for 4 to 5 sets of 10 to 25 repetitions of each exercise.

Wednesday Ab Exercises

This next day of abdominal work requires concentration, balance, and control.

Froggies

This movement is similar to the frog kick in the water.

1. Sit on the floor or on a chair. Keep your legs straight in front of you and your hands by your side. (Use only your fingertips for support in the

beginning; as you become stronger, you can do this movement without your hands as support.)

2. Lift your legs up off the floor.

3. Using your lower abdominals, slowly bend your knees and bring your feet inward toward your body.

4. Hold for 2 seconds, extend your legs again, and repeat.

Key Points to Remember

- Try not to touch the floor with your feet during your complete set.

- Do not lean back too much, as doing so will place stress on your back and turn the exercise into a hip-flexor movement rather than what it should be, a lower-abdominal exercise.

Follow this movement with the **crunches—butterfly position** and then **V sit-ups against the wall** for 4 to 5 sets of 10 to 25 repetitions of each exercise.

Photo 5.27
Froggies

Thursday Ab Exercises

Thursday's exercises build on familiar movements that now have a few variations for increased difficulty.

V Sit-Ups with a Medicine Ball

1. Lie on your back perpendicular to the wall, with your buttocks against the wall and your legs straight up and apart, with heels resting against the wall.

2. Hold a ball a few inches off the floor behind you. (Keep your arms bent.)

3. Raise the ball over your head, and curl up and touch the ball against the wall.

4. Hold for 2 seconds, lower to the starting position, and repeat.

Follow this movement with the **hip raises** and then the **seated knee-ups** for 4 to 5 sets of 10 to 25 repetitions of each exercise.

Photo 5.28
V Sit-Up with a Medicine Ball

Friday Ab Exercises

For this last day, you'll give your obliques, lower abdominals, and upper abdominals a good workout.

Bicycles

1. Lie on your back with your legs outstretched in front of you.

2. Place your hands on the back of your head, and raise your right elbow toward your left knee while bringing them together, twisting your upper body.

3. Hold for 2 seconds, and lie back down.

4. Draw your right leg in and bring your left elbow toward your right knee; hold, twist, and lower.

5. After doing 2 sets this way, raise your legs up to a 90 degree position (keeping your knees straight) and bring your elbows toward your knees without moving your legs.

Follow this movement with the **leg raises on your elbows** and then **hip raises** for 4 to 5 sets of 10 to 25 repetitions of each exercise.

Saturday and Sunday can be either rest days, if you want, or time to incorporate the first series of exercises into your routine.

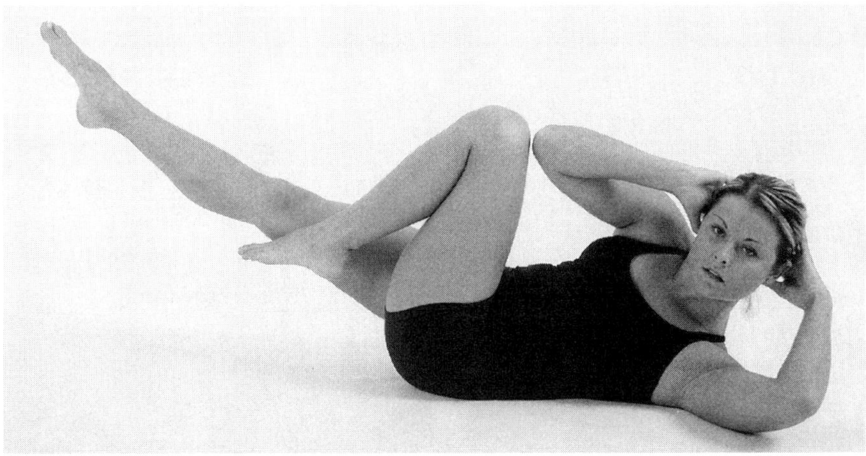

Photo 5.29
Bicycles

WHAT YOU WILL FIND FROM DOING ABDOMINAL WORK

At this point, you will see a more defined, stronger midsection, and you will notice less stiffness in your lower back with your newfound strength and flexibility. Begin interchanging the exercises throughout the week, and be creative with them. A pointer to keep in mind is not to overdo one region of the abdominal area within one workout; varying your emphasis is key to preventing injury to the lower back.

STAYING CHALLENGED WHILE PROTECTING YOUR BACK

Kate was a 31-year-old runner who had come in to see me because of chronic lower-back and leg pain during her runs. She said she used the weighted machine or a 10-pound plate across her chest when she worked her midsection. She said this was the only way she could feel her abdominals being worked.

After watching her do a few sets, I explained to her that she was hurting herself by placing a load in front of her spine as she did by holding the weights and that she was working her stomach region in a one-dimensional way. I showed her some of the intermediate and advanced movements that allowed her to be challenged but also worked all sides of her abdominal region more effectively.

Two months later on her follow-up visit, she said she was working her abdominals more frequently and had less pain since starting the BackSmart program.

To have a flat, strong abdominal region, remember that you must maintain a proper body position throughout your exercises and use as many movements as possible on different days. Also, working the stomach muscles from different angles and intensity levels throughout the week will assure you a strong and supportive midsection, which is important for spinal control and lifting motions. Now let's move on to the ball in the next chapter to further sculpt and define your physique while preventing injuries.

CHAPTER 6

BALL AND BALANCE DRILLS TO KEEP YOU STRONG AND STEADY

As people age, they lose elasticity in their joints and muscles, resulting in rigidity of movement. This, in turn, causes people to lose their balance—while stepping off of curbs or simply moving around their homes. A number of things can affect your sense of balance as you age. A vision problem or a condition such as arthritis can make you less secure on your feet. Side effects of medications are another common cause of imbalance.

WORKING OUT WITH THE SWISS BALL

Using the physio ball, commonly known as the Swiss ball, is a fun, challenging, and innovative way to exercise. The Swiss ball can be used not only to improve muscle control but also to increase balance, strength, and flexibility beyond the normal workout. It forces users to maintain balance and control during their movements, while also providing an effective muscular workout. Traditional exercises (such as those using machines or free weights that isolate your muscles rather than forcing them to work as a unit) often ignore the core muscles that are needed for stability. Working on the ball releases muscle tension as it restores rhythm between the brain and the body.

You can add a ball workout twice a week, or try to incorporate a ball routine into your daily workout. The following routines in this chapter are divided into lower- and upper-body workouts. With the more advanced exercises, you can incorporate cables and free weights into your regular weight-training routine.

Benefits of Using the Swiss Ball

In addition to developing a strong midsection and a lean, toned body, you'll find other benefits of incorporating the ball into your workout routine.

- **Improved posture.** Your posture will be much better because you are maintaining the lumbar natural curve in the lower back.
- **Abdominal/core stability.** The Swiss ball targets the deep abdominals and deep back erector muscles that stabilize and support the spine, thus providing you with support for movements such as lifting, running, and throwing. Strengthening the muscles that stabilize the spine reduces the risk of future injury.
- **Muscle balance.** All muscle groups have an opposing muscle: triceps and biceps are an example. If one muscle is stronger than its counterpart, muscle imbalance occurs. There is also a tendency for the stronger muscle to be tighter. Over time, this tightness can create problems such as pulled muscles and poor posture, increasing the likelihood of repeated injuries.
- **Flexibility and mobility.** The Swiss ball relieves joint stiffness and tight muscles, which create limitations in movement and compromise posture. Both can contribute to pain and increases of injury.
- **Relaxation in the body.** The natural motion that occurs while you use the ball can stretch and relax your body, preventing muscle tightness and joint stiffness. This improves your quality of movement and decreases the risk of injury.

IMPROVING COORDINATION AND BALANCE WITH BALL EXERCISES

Duncan, a 53-year-old former competitive fencer, taught fencing two nights a week. He had always worked out and kept in shape. He slipped on a patch of ice during the winter and hurt the right side of his body, from the neck all the way down to his knee. Three months later, he still felt sore and stiff, so he came to me for help.

I introduced him to the ball exercises, which he found challenging. He said he felt that he had regained his coordination and had more balance in his fencing stances as a result of using the BackSmart program. His aches and pains diminished, and he has moved on to the intermediate level. He also has his fencing club doing the BackSmart stretches and balance drills.

Choosing the Right Ball Size

Before you begin, it's important to make sure you have the right ball for your height, since that will affect your form as you complete these exercises.

A general rule is to use a ball that allows you to sit on it with your hips and knees bent at 90-degree angles. Use the following table as a guideline:

Swiss Ball Size	Your Height
45 cm	Use if you are less than 5′ tall
55 cm	Use if you are 5′ to 5′8″
65 cm	Use if you are 5′9″ to 6′2″
75 cm	Use if you are taller than 6′2″

How to Stay Balanced

Here are a few hints that will help you keep your balance on the ball as you perform the exercises in this chapter.

- Do the exercises barefoot at first, and as you progress, you can do them wearing shoes if you like.

- Use your breathing to help stabilize your body throughout each movement.

- Push down through your feet for better control while performing these movements.

- Stay focused and pull in your abdominal muscles throughout the exercises.

When learning each of these Swiss ball movements, use the following list as a guide for the number of sets and reps:

- **Beginner.** 2 to 3 sets of 10 repetitions.
- **Intermediate.** 3 to 4 sets of 10 to 15 repetitions.
- **Advanced.** 4 to 5 sets of 15 to 20 repetitions.

LOWER-BODY BALL WORKOUT

Your core region consists of many deep frontal and posterior muscles along the spine and abdominal regions. By working these muscle groups together, you will enhance your overall body control and help prevent injuries.

Single-Hamstring Lift

1. Get into the same position as for the **hip raises** (lying on your back, toes pointed), with your feet on the ball.

2. Keep one leg straight and exhale as you raise the other leg toward the ceiling.

Photo 6.1
Single-Hamstring Lift

3. Inhale and lower your leg.

4. Complete a set on one side; then switch and repeat the exercise with the other leg.

Swiss Ball Crunch

1. Lie back on the ball with your upper body over the ball and your feet shoulder-width apart on the floor. Keep your head relaxed downward and your hands on the back of your head.

2. Contract your abdominal muscles and exhale as you slowly curl your shoulders forward and toward your hips (or as far as you can go).

3. Hold for 2 seconds at the top of the movement.

4. Inhale as you return to the starting position, and repeat.

Photo 6.2
Swiss Ball Crunch

Key Points to Remember

- Start the exercise with your head back far enough to feel a slight stretch in your abdominals.
- Curl up as high as you can.

Side-Lying Airplane Roll

This next exercise uses coordination and balance while strengthening the oblique muscle groups along the side of your waist.

1. Lie with your back on top of the ball and your hips off the ball.
2. With your feet placed firmly on the floor and your knees bent, extend both arms out straight at your sides. (Form a bridge, so that your hips are high and parallel to your chest.)

Photo 6.3
Side-Lying Airplane Roll

3. Exhale and slowly roll to the right, trying to touch the floor with your right hand while raising your left arm.

4. Inhale as you return to the starting position, and repeat on the other side.

Ball Pull-In

In addition to improving balance and coordination, this exercise will help strengthen your chest, shoulders, arms, and abdominals.

1. Start in the push-up position, with your lower shins on top of the ball and toes pointed away from your head.

2. Keeping your back straight and tight throughout the movement, exhale as you slowly pull your knees in toward your chest, allowing the ball to roll forward.

3. Pause for 2 seconds, and then contract your abdominals at the end of the movement.

4. Inhale as you straighten your legs, rolling the ball back to the beginning position.

Photos 6.4, 6.5 Ball Pull-In

For a Challenge

You can also do the following variations, which will stimulate more abdominal involvement:

- Rest only your toes on the ball.
- Keep your chin down toward your chest during the entire movement.

Swiss Ball Leg Raise

1. Lie on your back with your upper body stretched out across the ball and your arms overhead, holding on to something (such as a workout bench) behind you.
2. Raise your feet off the floor with a slight bend in your knees.
3. Contract your abdominals, and exhale as you lift and curl your hips toward your shoulders until your feet are pointing up.
4. Inhale as you slowly lower your legs to the starting position without touching the floor with your feet, and repeat.

Photos 6.6, 6.7 Swiss Ball Leg Raise

Key Points to Remember
The more you can concentrate and contract your abdominals while lowering your legs slowly, the more you will enhance your strength and control.

UPPER-BODY BALL WORKOUT

Now that you have warmed up your middle to lower half, it is time to move to the upper body. By incorporating dumbbells in some of the next exercises, you will improve your overall strength much faster, sculpting your body while enhancing your coordination. You should use a lighter weight (no more than 20-pound dumbbells is a good rule to follow) than you would normally use for these movements if you were not on a ball. The reason is that you will not only be lifting weights but also focusing on balance.

Arm Rollout

This exercise will work the arms, chest, shoulders, abdominals, and upper back while challenging balance and coordination.

1. Kneel in front of the ball, and place your hands on top of the ball, with only a slight bend in your elbows.

2. Exhale and slowly allow the ball to roll forward as far as you can go. (The goal is for your upper body to be parallel to the floor.)

Photo 6.8
Arm Rollout

3. Pause for 2 seconds, inhale as you return to the starting position, and repeat.

For a Challenge

Try starting from a standing position and then begin to roll out.

Handstand

This exercise works the shoulders, arms, upper back, chest, and abdominals.

1. Start in the push-up position (as you did for **ball pull-ins**), with your toes on top of the ball and your hands on the floor. Keep your back and legs straight.

2. Exhale as you slowly pull your feet in toward your hands, causing the ball to roll forward, until your hips are raised and you are in a "partial" handstand. (Most of your weight will be on your hands, and your hips will be the highest part of your body.)

Photo 6.9
Handstand

3. Pause for 2 seconds, and contract your abdominals at the end of the movement.

4. Inhale and move your legs back to the starting position, pause for a few moments, and repeat.

Biceps Curl

This exercise emphasizes biceps, forearms, and shoulders, but because it's done on the ball, it also helps develop coordination and balance throughout your body.

1. Sit on the ball, with your feet planted firmly on the floor. Hold a dumbbell in each hand, with your arms straight down at your sides.

2. Exhale and slowly curl your hands up toward your shoulders, and squeeze your biceps at the end of the movement.

Photo 6.10
Biceps Curl

3. Hold for 2 seconds, inhale as you lower to the starting position, and repeat.

For a Challenge

If you're at the advanced level, you can perform the last set while lying flat on the ball, which will create a stronger stretch in the arms.

Triceps Kickback

This next exercise works the important and often ignored triceps as well as the shoulders and chest.

1. Lie prone over the ball, with the balls of your feet on the floor and your chest slightly raised. Hold your weights by your hips, with elbows high and close to your sides.
2. Exhale and straighten your arms, pressing the weights toward the ceiling.
3. Inhale and bend your elbows to lower your hands back to the ball.

Photo 6.11
Triceps Kickback

Photo 6.12
Pull-Over

Pull-Over

This next exercise is a unique way of incorporating the BackSmart principles by not stressing the spine while working the shoulder and back muscles from different angles.

1. Lie on your back on the ball, and hold a dumbbell with both hands behind your head.

2. Exhale and slowly move your arms forward, pulling the dumbbell down toward your feet. (Drop your hips as you roll forward.)

3. Inhale as you return to the starting position, and repeat.

Hand Walking

It's important to pull your stomach in and breathe in a steady fashion throughout this movement.

1. Lie on your stomach, centered over the ball, with your hands on the floor in front of you and your feet together on the floor behind you.

2. Walk your hands forward one at a time, allowing the ball to slide along your legs until just your feet are resting on the ball.

3. Walk your hands backward to the starting position, and repeat.

Photo 6.13
Hand Walking

Reverse Bridge

This last exercise in the series should be done slowly to emphasize balance and control.

1. Sit on the floor, with your back on the ball, your knees bent, and your feet shoulder-width apart.
2. Lean back slightly (45 degrees or less) and put your hands on the floor.

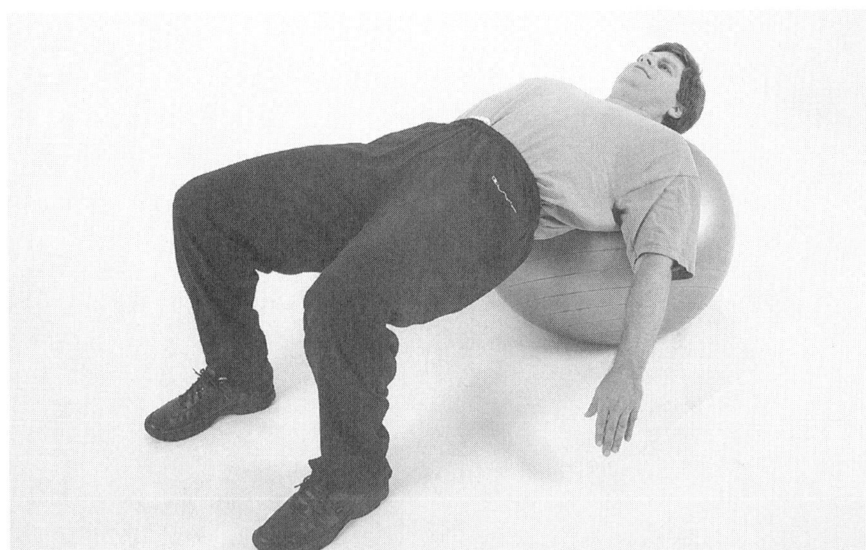

Photo 6.14
Reverse Bridge

3. Exhale and slowly lift your upper body until it is parallel to the floor.

4. Hold for 2 seconds, inhale as you slowly lower to the starting position, and repeat.

HOW THE BACKSMART BALL WORKOUT CAN HELP REDUCE BACK AND NECK PAIN

Sherry, a 27-year-old computer programmer who worked a lot of overtime, spent far too many hours in front of a computer screen. She started and stopped numerous diets and exercise programs, never staying with them for long because her work would eat up all her waking hours, as she put it. She developed headaches and neck and back strain as a result of her posture at her workstation.

A friend referred her to the center for her headaches and pain. After listening to her history, I brought out the Swiss ball and asked her if she would use this practical and effective tool at her office. At first she was reluctant, but after suffering another sleepless night from her pain, she slowly began using the ball on her lunch breaks and during the afterwork hours.

Within a short time, she started to feel the results. She now does the BackSmart ball routine three to four times per week and has bought an extra ball to use at home on the weekends.

When you train on the ball, every time the ball moves, you must activate muscles deep in your back, stomach, and hips to stabilize yourself. In this way, you create a stronger, more functional, athletic body.

Now that you have been doing challenging exercises that strengthen your core and help your coordination and control, you're primed to move on to some balance drills to improve your coordination.

BALANCE DRILLS TO KEEP YOU STEADY ON YOUR FEET

The exercises in this next section are designed to enhance your balance with challenging movements that can be performed with eyes open or closed. Since the eyes are the primary source of balance, sensory input, and awareness of surroundings, the advantage to performing these exercises with your eyes closed is that your brain is forced to rely on other sensory inputs. For example, when you're balancing on one leg with your eyes closed, your body relies on mechanical receptors in the lower leg joints to maintain balance. The brain receives information from these mechanical receptors, which are now the predominant sensors for balance and coordination, rather than from the visual sensors. The brain then sends instructions to the rest of the body about how, why, and when to react.

With these techniques, you can develop an awareness of the body's natural amount of sway, to help you balance. Sway happens constantly while you're standing, walking, and working out. With a little training, anyone can improve his or her balance and fitness level.

Benefits of Balance Exercises

Balance drills will change the way you feel, move, and look for the rest of your life. These exercises will do this because they were developed to first restore your alignment and then balance muscle flexibility and, ultimately, strengthen your body. These sequences of flowing movements that will have you alternately bending and stretching forward, backward, and toward the sides will elongate everything that tends to shorten and strengthen everything that tends to weaken, thus making you both supple and strong.

Doing these exercises will also give you complete control of your coordination as you build a stronger consciousness of your center. Not only will you feel great as your posture straightens and you get stronger, but you'll look great too. You will begin to move more freely as your joints become more adapted to your environment and thus lessen the stress you put on your body.

A WELL-BALANCED WORKOUT

I will explain in detail how to improve your body awareness and stabilization of your spine. As you spend a few minutes a day performing these balancing tasks, you will immediately notice an improved ability to sense imbalance and will be able to recover more quickly when balance is lost; this translates into injury prevention.

People with better balance respond to training and learn sports skills more quickly. There is a strong link between reaction-time movement and balance.

You can do these exercises as often as you like, to stimulate your muscles and the nerve communication on which you rely for coordination. All of these exercises should be performed barefoot and can be done in the comfort of your home, taking between 10 and 15 minutes a day. When learning these balance movements, people at all levels should complete each exercise as follows: 2 to 4 sets of 10 to 15 repetitions.

Standing Asleep

1. Stand with your feet together. Keep your arms by your sides or rest your hands on your waist.

2. Slowly bend your left knee and raise it to waist height or higher. Point your toes down throughout the movement, and continually look forward, not down.

Photo 6.15
Standing Asleep

3. Hold the position for 10 seconds at first, and then for 20 seconds and longer, until you are up to a full minute.

4. Slowly lower your leg, and repeat with your other leg.

For a Challenge

If you are more advanced, you can start by closing one eye while lifting the leg on that side of your body. Then close the eye on the opposite side of the leg being lifted, and progress to closing both eyes during the movement.

Key Points to Remember

- Breathe normally with your stomach, not with your chest, keeping your center low.

- Concentrate on balancing yourself without rocking side-to-side or forward and backward.

Front Kick

1. Start in the same position as for **standing asleep**, raising your bent left knee toward your waist; hold for 2 seconds.

2. Slowly extend the leg, with toes flexed, until it is locked. Your toes should remain flexed throughout the movement.

3. Hold this position for 2 seconds, slowly bring your foot back until your knee is at waist height, and repeat without touching the floor. Then switch to the other side and repeat.

BackSmart Alternative

You can use a chair or stand next to a wall, and place one or two fingers on the chair or wall for support, until you gain more balance.

Photo 6.16
Front Kick

Exercise Back Kick

This more advanced movement will challenge your balance and improve your coordination tremendously. A common mistake that people make when performing this movement is leaning too far forward or tipping to the side at the end of the kick positions. Try to stay as upright as possible. This is a balance drill as well as a great leg and hip workout. As you gain strength and flexibility, you will be able to raise your foot higher in the kick positions.

1. Start in same position as for the front kick—raising your left leg, with your knee bent.

2. Complete one front kick as explained in the previous exercise.

3. Bring your leg back and rotate it out toward the side without dropping your knee position.

4. Slowly extend your leg backward, holding the extended position for 2 seconds, and then bring it in slowly.

5. Keep your knee up as you swing your leg around, so your knee is in front of your stomach.

6. Slowly lower your leg toward the floor, touch your foot lightly down, and repeat.

7. Switch legs after doing 1 set on one side.

BackSmart Alternative
Use a chair or wall at the beginning to help with balance.

Photos 6.17, 6.18 Exercise Back Kick

Exercise Pike Position

1. Stand with your feet together, bend at the waist, and extend your left arm in front of you.

2. While still bending at the waist, raise your right leg behind you. (In the finished position, you are outstretched with the leg completely extended waist high.)

3. Remain looking straight ahead. Bend at the waist, keeping your upper body straight while looking ahead, and hold this position for 20 to 30 seconds. Then repeat with the opposite arm and leg.

For a Challenge

As you improve your balance, try these advanced alternatives:

- Tilt your head upward and twist your upper body, lifting your right hand toward the ceiling and extending as high as possible while maintaining your balance. Hold for 2 seconds, and then repeat with the opposite leg.

- For an even more advanced workout, do it with light hand weights—forcing your body to adapt to the increased difficulty.

Photo 6.19
Exercise Pike Position

Figure-4 One-Legged Squat

1. Stand erect with your hands on your hips, and shift your weight to your right foot.

2. Lift your left knee and place your left ankle across your right thigh so that your left knee turns out.

3. Contract your abdominals and drop your hips to maintain the upright, balanced position.

4. Bend your right knee to sit back into a one-legged squat.

5. Hold for 2 seconds, rise up to the starting position, and repeat with the opposite leg.

Photo 6.20
Figure-4
One-Legged Squat

Kneeling on the Ball

Returning now to the Swiss ball, you will not only develop a greater sense of balance and coordination but also have complete control of your deep muscle groups in your abdominal and lower-back regions. Once you accomplish these challenging movements, you will truly find your center and further prevent injuries from occurring while improving your athletic ability.

1. Start with the ball in front of you, resting between your knees. Reach forward and place your fingertips on the back of a chair for support.

2. Slowly roll up onto the ball with your knees, holding the back of the chair as you roll forward.

Photo 6.21
Kneeling on the Ball

3. Contract your midsection and lower-back regions, stabilizing your body over the center of the ball. Concentrate on a relaxed breathing pattern as you focus on a distance point on the far wall.

4. Release one hand and slowly raise it in front of your chest.

5. Release your opposite hand and bring it up even with the other hand in front of your body.

6. Hold for as long as possible, trying to achieve 30 seconds to a minute.

Leaning-Tower Stance with Ball

This last balance exercise is an advanced posture. I consider this movement one of the more challenging of all. As you develop your sense of balance, you will strengthen and tone your abdominal muscles while improving your posture.

1. Stand with your feet shoulder-distance apart. Find a relaxed posture, with your head straight and looking forward.

2. Pick up the Swiss ball and hold it in front of you at arms' length.

Photo 6.22
Leaning-Tower Stance with Ball

3. Slowly exhale and contract your abdominal muscles, holding your spine in a neutral position.

4. Lean slightly forward and extend your arms as you press your right leg out behind you about 8 to 10 inches.

5. Hold this position for 10 to 20 seconds, breathing rhythmically.

6. Slowly return to the starting position, and release your arms toward your body as you place your extended leg on the floor again.

7. Repeat on the other side.

For a Challenge

From the same starting position, extend your arms and raise the ball overhead as you flex at the hips, and lean forward until your upper body and leg are parallel to the floor.

IMPROVING POSTURE AND COORDINATION

Esther, a 60-year-old former competitive ice-skater, said that, in her prime, she had the grace of a ballerina. But now, after years of injuries and arthritic pain, she was unable to exercise without considerable pain.

She began using the stretches and progressed to the BackSmart balance movements. She immediately noticed an improvement in her posture, and the body control she once had came back quickly with daily use. She tripped less often and felt less stiff and sore after performing the movements. She said she actually could feel her stomach muscles working again.

As you can see, by completing these movements, not only will you remain steady on your feet, but also you will have improved your body awareness and stabilization of your spine. You will excel at your other activities, from golf or tennis to any other movement that requires you to have hand-eye coordination, because you have maintained the elasticity in your joints and muscles, aiding in your balance, regardless of your age, resulting in injury prevention.

CHAPTER 7

HOME SWEET HOME WORKOUT

There is no better place to work out than your own home. As shown in the previous three chapters, numerous exercises can be done without any special equipment or distractions typical of a loud gym environment.

You will now continue strengthening the body, this time isolating individual body parts. As you proceed, remember that a workout should not harm your body! Having stated that, I want you to be prepared to have a challenging, effective, and fun workout. I will provide instruction for isolating muscles using chairs, stairs, and your body weight and lifting dumbbells, in either the home or the gym. These BackSmart techniques will result in stronger, shapelier muscles without causing back injury. Reshaping the body by enhancing muscles will also burn off the fat! Waking up with back pain will no longer be an excuse to avoid exercise. This chapter will show you the effective use of the wall or lying on the floor to enhance your workouts without additional strain to back muscles.

BENEFITS OF WORKING OUT AT HOME

Doing a workout at home is convenient as well as less distracting than the gym. You can stay focused and go at your own pace, not someone else's, during your exercise routine. One of the main reasons you should do the at-home workout is that you can incorporate more of the stretching workout into your weight regimen.

I had a patient in her mid-forties who told me that she would often hire a personal trainer to teach her the exercises and would end up hurting herself, barely able to get out of bed the next day, and as a result, she swore off all forms of resistance exercises. After explaining all the benefits of weight training, such as increased bone density, improved circulation, and enhanced muscular endurance, I told her it also helps speed up the body's metabolism, hence creating a fat-burning, leaner, healthier body. I described the following set of exercises that could be done in the privacy of her home to improve her posture and strengthen the muscles of her spine.

Remember, no one is watching, and you do not need heavy weights to get results. On the contrary, I want you to start out with light weights to concentrate on the muscles being worked and focus in on the spinal muscles and abdominal muscles.

SETTING UP YOUR HOME GYM

To get ready for these exercises, you'll want to make sure that you have all the equipment you'll need and that you have a few basic concepts down.

Equipment You Will Need

You'll need the following equipment in order to complete the exercises:

- **Dumbbells.** Get a few sets of dumbbells ranging from 3 pounds to 35 pounds, depending on your level. Two or three sets should be good for a start; you can always add more later.

- **Workout bench.** Make sure you have a bench that is strong enough to support you. If you don't have a bench on which to lie, you can substitute chairs.

- **Chairs.** Use two (or three) strong straight-back chairs that will support your weight.

- **Medicine ball.** You'll be using the ball for the leg workout, so choose one that weighs from 4 to 6 pounds to begin with.

Focusing on Form and Breathing

Putting these basic concepts into practice will help you as you execute the exercises in this chapter.

- Focus on the muscles and the way they feel, not the amount of weight you can lift.
- Pay attention to your posture throughout the exercises.
- Remember to pull in your abdominal muscles during all the exercises to help stabilize your spine.
- Breathe deeply and relax during and after a set of exercises; do not hold your breath when lifting weights. Instead, focus on emptying your lungs on each exhale.

WORKING ON DIFFERENT MUSCLE GROUPS

I've divided this chapter into specific muscle groups that you'll be working with each set of exercises. Beginners should follow the order of exercises presented here to help with posture and strengthen the back muscles without placing stress on the spine. You will start off warming up the back and then move to a standing position against the wall, helping your body to adapt to a stronger back position without sacrificing form, while giving you better control of the movements. You will end the series of exercises by lying down and isolating the lower-back muscles, thus further preventing injuries to the spine while enhancing your athletic body.

IMPORTANCE OF INCORPORATING WEIGHTS INTO YOUR WORKOUT

Rachel, a 46-year-old salesperson, spent a lot of time on the phone in her home office. She would take breaks in the course of the day to eat and walk her dog. She said she couldn't work out with an exercise tape because it would take too long. She needed an alternative because a bone density study showed that she had early signs of osteoporosis, and weight training was recommended to help fight this process.

I started her off with the BackSmart at-home workout program because it fit her schedule and she felt she could break it up throughout the day without losing any time commuting back and forth to a gym.

Within two months, she had lost eight pounds, and she now works the BackSmart program into her day four times per week. She has reduced her stress and feels better.

WORKING AT YOUR OWN LEVEL

A general rule for choosing the right amount of weight for your exercises is to first use a weight that you can lift only about five times, making this your max weight. Calculate 50 percent, 60 percent, and 70 percent of that number, and you have the amount of weight with which to start as you do your reps. For example, let's say you can curl 50 pounds for 5 repetitions. For your first sets, you would use 25 pounds, your second would be 30 pounds, and your third and last set would be 35 pounds. Remember that this is a general guideline; people who are much stronger will start with heavier weights, while others will start with lighter weights.

When trying these exercises, start with light weights until you are comfortable with the movements, and gradually add weight as you become stronger. When you can complete 3 sets of 12 to 15 repetitions consistently for two workouts, you can probably start adding weight by 2 to 5 pounds to your exercises.

When learning each of the at-home exercises in this chapter, use the following list as a guide for the number of sets and reps:

- **Beginner.** 2 to 3 sets of 10 repetitions.
- **Intermediate.** 3 to 4 sets of 12 to 15 repetitions.
- **Advanced.** 4 to 5 sets of 12 to 20 repetitions.

BACK MUSCLES

The first set of exercises will strengthen the back. You'll need a workout bench, or two chairs, and a dumbbell.

Dumbbell Pull-Over

1. Lie on your back on the bench or across two chairs.

2. Lift the dumbbell overhead, and hold it with your arms slightly bent straight above your chest.

3. Inhale deeply as you slowly lower the weight in an arc behind your head. (You will feel an intense stretch in your chest and back muscles.)

4. Hold for 2 seconds, and then exhale as you pull your arms back to the starting position, and repeat.

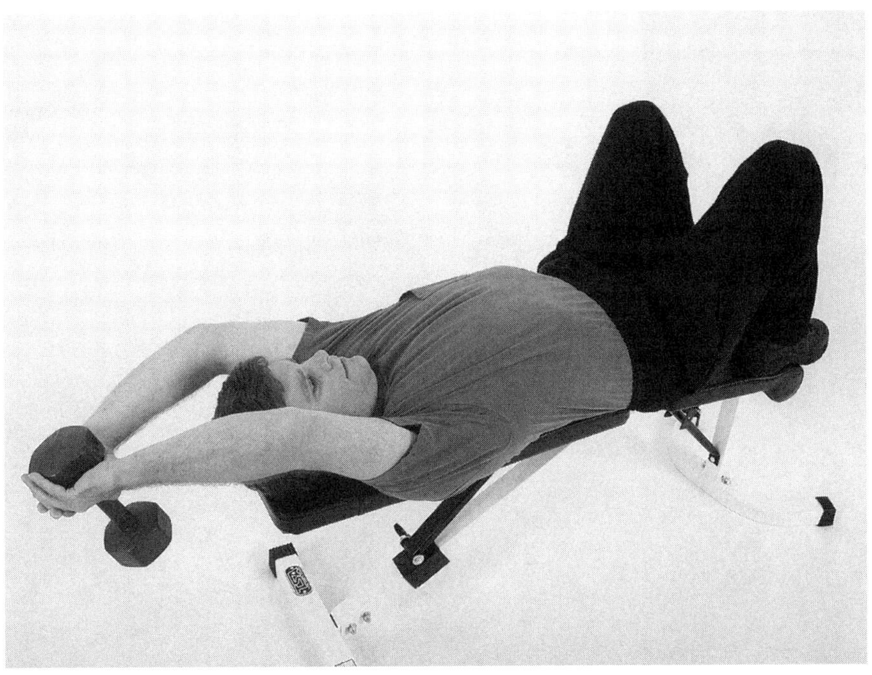

Photo 7.1
Dumbbell Pull-Over

Dumbbell Row

For this next exercise, it's important that you do not round your back and that you look straight down in order to prevent neck strain.

1. Place your left foot flat on the floor, and rest your right knee on the workout bench or on a chair seat for support.

2. Lean forward at the waist while holding a dumbbell in your left hand, using your right hand for support by placing it on the bench or chair in front of your knee. (Your upper body should be parallel to the floor.)

3. Inhale, and slowly pull the dumbbell up along your left side until your hand is alongside your ribs.

4. Squeeze your back muscles for 2 seconds, exhale as you lower the weight to the starting position, and repeat.

5. After completing the sets, switch to the other side and repeat the exercise.

Photo 7.2
Dumbbell Row

BICEPS WORKOUT

The next set of exercises will help to sculpt and define the arms in a safe and effective way that does not harm your back.

Wall/Arm Curl

If you are stiff and sore, and bending over aggravates your back, you can do this exercise in a chair instead of against the wall, to reduce stress to your back muscles.

1. Lean your back against the wall, with your arms down by your sides, holding a dumbbell in each hand.

2. Inhale, and slowly curl the dumbbells up toward your shoulders. Your palms should be up throughout the movement.

3. Exhale as you slowly return the dumbbells to the starting position, and repeat.

Photo 7.3
Wall/Arm Curl

One-Arm Curl, Holding the Wall

1. Stand facing the wall, and bend over slightly, resting one hand on the wall to stabilize yourself.

2. Hold a dumbbell in your other hand, allowing your arm to hang freely.

3. Inhale, and curl the weight up to your shoulder without moving your upper arm or elbow. (As you lift, twist your wrist so that your little finger ends up higher than your thumb.)

4. Flex and contract the muscle at the top of the movement and hold for 2 seconds.

5. Exhale as you slowly lower the weight to the starting position, and repeat.

6. After completing the sets, switch to the other arm and repeat the exercise.

Photo 7.4
One-Arm Curl, Holding the Wall

SHOULDER WORKOUT

The use of the wall is an effective training tool for isolating the shoulder region. If your back is sore, you'll find that this exercise will give it great support, helping you to focus on the muscles during the workout.

Dumbbell Press Against the Wall

For this next exercise, make sure you are pushing your back against the wall as you lift and lower your arms.

1. Squat, with your legs parallel to the floor, your feet shoulder-width apart, and your back flat against the wall.

2. Hold a dumbbell in each hand, and raise the weights to shoulder height, keeping your elbows out to the sides and your palms facing forward.

Photo 7.5 Dumbbell Press Against the Wall

3. Inhale, and lift the dumbbells straight up until they touch at the top.

4. Exhale as you lower the weights as far as possible, and repeat.

Lateral Raise

If you're doing this next exercise right, after the overhead pressing movement, you will probably feel your thigh muscles start to shake. This is fine, as it will build more endurance into your legs as a bonus to working your shoulders. As with the previous exercise, make sure you are pushing your back against the wall as you lift and lower your arms.

1. Begin in the same position as for the dumbbell press against the wall (squatting with legs parallel to the floor, feet shoulder-width apart, and your back flat against the wall, holding a dumbbell in each hand).

2. Bend your elbows slightly and lift the weights out and up to either side, turning your wrists slightly (as if you're pouring water out of a pitcher) so that the rear of the dumbbells is higher than the front.

Photo 7.6
Lateral Raise

3. Inhale, and lift the weights slightly higher than your shoulders; hold for 2 seconds.

4. Exhale as you lower the weights slowly to the starting position, and repeat.

Bent-Over Lateral Raise

For this last shoulder exercise, you may want to place a towel between your head and the wall for comfort. When performing this exercise, be careful not to lift your body as you lift the weights. Your body should remain steady throughout the movement.

1. Stand facing the wall, two to three feet away, and slowly bend forward from the waist; rest your head against the wall so that your upper body is parallel to the floor.

2. Hold a dumbbell in each hand, and turn them so that your palms face each other.

3. Lift the weights out to either side, turning each wrist so that the thumb is lower than the little finger.

Photo 7.7
Bent-Over Lateral Raise

4. With your arms slightly bent, inhale, and lift the dumbbells just higher than your head; hold for 2 seconds.

5. Exhale as you slowly lower the weights to the beginning position, and repeat.

TRICEPS WORKOUT

This next set of exercises will work the triceps muscles, further sculpting and defining the arms.

Dumbbell Kickback

For this exercise, you can hold on to the back of a chair or lean against a wall for support.

1. Bend your torso forward at the waist, and place one hand on either the wall or a chair for balance.

2. Holding a dumbbell in the other hand, bend your elbow about 90 degrees from the starting position.

Photo 7.8
Dumbbell Kickback

3. Inhale, and extend your arm fully.

4. Exhale as you slowly return the weight to the starting position, and repeat.

Dip with Chair Seats

This last triceps exercise should be done utilizing a slow and controlled movement.

1. Stand between two chairs, with the seats facing each other and your back to the chairs.

2. Place your hands in the center of the chair seats slightly behind you, with your feet out in front, resting on your heels.

3. Bend your elbows and inhale as you slowly lower your buttocks to touch the floor.

4. Exhale as you press up to the starting position, and repeat.

Photo 7.9
Dip with Chair Seats

CHEST WORKOUT

The home workout is one of the more effective ways of working out with little use of space and time. This set of exercises will work your entire chest area without putting unwanted stress on your joints and tendons. The accompanying tips give you ideas on how to increase the intensity and avoid common pitfalls associated with these movements.

Basic Push-Up

If you haven't done push-ups in a while, start off slowly on your knees, and then go to one knee while the other leg is straight, before doing them on your feet with both legs straight. It's more important to do more reps than to see how heavy a weight you can lift, at the beginning.

1. Start with your hands and your feet shoulder-width apart.

2. Inhale as you push yourself up until your arms are completely locked out, and hold for 2 seconds.

3. Exhale as you slowly lower yourself, with control, until your chest touches the floor.

4. Press yourself back up and repeat.

Photo 7.10
Basic Push-Up

Photo 7.11
Bench or Stair Push-Up

Bench or Stair Push-Up

Once you have got comfortable with basic push-ups, you can do them with your feet on a bench, chair, or stair. By elevating your body this way, you will increase the intensity of the exercise and build a tremendous amount of endurance in the arms and shoulders.

If you are using stairs, start at the bottom stair, and with each progressive set, go up one stair. When you reach the top stair, come back down with each set.

LEG WORKOUT

The following exercises work the leg muscles using a medicine ball, dumbbells, and your own weight as resistance.

Karate Front Stance

This exercise develops mobility, flexibility, and balance.

1. Stand with your feet together and your hands resting on your waist.

2. Bend your right knee as you glide your right foot forward until your feet are shoulder-width apart, placing most of your body weight on the bent front leg. (Keep your back leg straight and your feet pointing forward, so you will feel the stretch in the back leg and your quad muscles in the front leg.)

Photo 7.12
Karate Front Stance

3. Pull your back leg toward your front leg, bending your knees as you bring them together, keeping your center low.

4. Glide your left foot forward and repeat the exercise; continue alternating legs while walking forward.

For a Challenge

As you get better, try doing some karate stances while gliding your legs backward. This will work your muscles from a different angle.

Side Squat

This exercise will work your inner- and outer-thigh area, while improving your balance.

Photo 7.13
Side Squat

1. Stand with your feet slightly wider than shoulder-width apart.

2. Raise your arms out in front of you to help with your balance. (Keep your head up, and focus on a distant point in front of you.)

3. Slowly bend your right knee and exhale as you squat, keeping your left leg straight.

4. Inhale as you slowly rise, switch to the opposite side, and repeat.

BackSmart Alternative
If you are not as flexible, you can use a chair in front of you to help with your balance and coordination until you can perform these squats without it.

Chair Squat

For this next exercise, you can work the muscle groups from different angles by slowly moving your feet closer together with each set until they are touching.

1. Stand in front of the chair (approximately 2 to 3 inches away), with your back toward the chair and your feet shoulder-width apart. Your arms can be used for balance by placing them in front of you.

2. Using your body weight, bend your legs and exhale as you lower your hips until you touch the chair slightly.

3. Inhale as you rise, return to the starting position, and repeat.

For a Challenge

To stimulate more muscle groups in the process, you can do the following variations:

- Stand behind the chair and lower yourself farther.

- Hold a dumbbell in each hand as you perform this exercise.

Photo 7.14
Chair Squat

INNER-THIGH WORKOUT

Many people concentrate on their inner and outer thighs by working them on specific machines at the gym or lying on the floor and doing hour after hour of leg kicks. These types of exercises usually overstress the gluteus medius, a side buttocks muscle. While the machines at the gyms stress these areas, they also put a large amount of stress on the sacroiliac joints along the back of the hips, which may lead to lower-back problems.

So instead, I have isolated a group of challenging exercises to stimulate the muscle fibers while burning calories. These muscle groups help in many sports and other weight-training movements by stabilizing and strengthening the lower core muscle groups, thus preventing lower-back pain. Using a medicine ball for these movements is ideal. However, if you do not have one available, you can use a basketball or volleyball instead.

Two-Leg Lift with Ball Between Knees

In this next exercise, you will feel your inner thighs and gluteus muscles extensively.

1. Lie on your back with your feet on the floor, holding the ball between your bent knees.

2. Inhale as you raise your buttocks as high as five inches off the floor, and squeeze the ball at the top for 5 seconds.

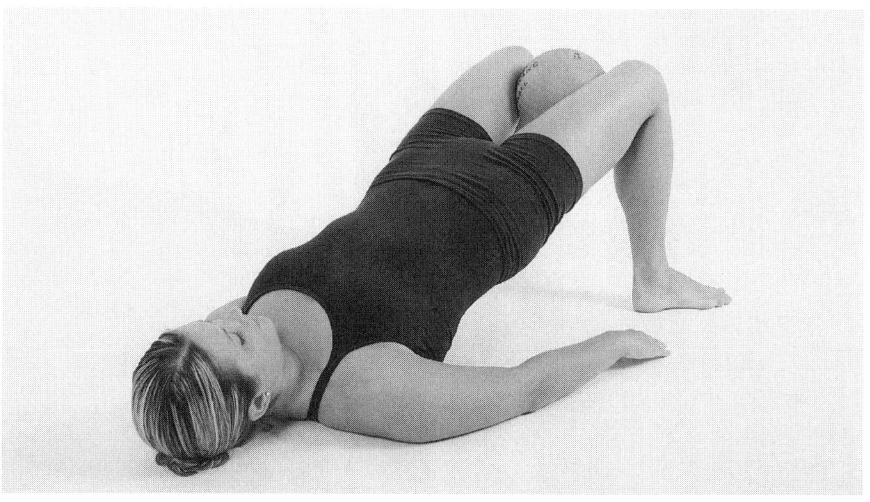

Photo 7.15
Two-Leg Lift with Ball Between Knees

3. Exhale as you release, lower your buttocks, and repeat.

BackSmart Alternative

Keep your lower back flat against the floor during the entire exercise as you squeeze the ball, hold for 5 seconds, relax, and repeat.

One-Leg Lift

1. As in the previous exercise, lie on your back with your feet on the floor, holding the ball between your bent knees.

2. Inhale, and raise one leg while squeezing the ball between your knees.

3. Hold for 5 seconds, and exhale as you lower your leg.

4. Complete 10 repetitions, switch to the opposite leg, and repeat.

Photo 7.16
One-Leg Lift

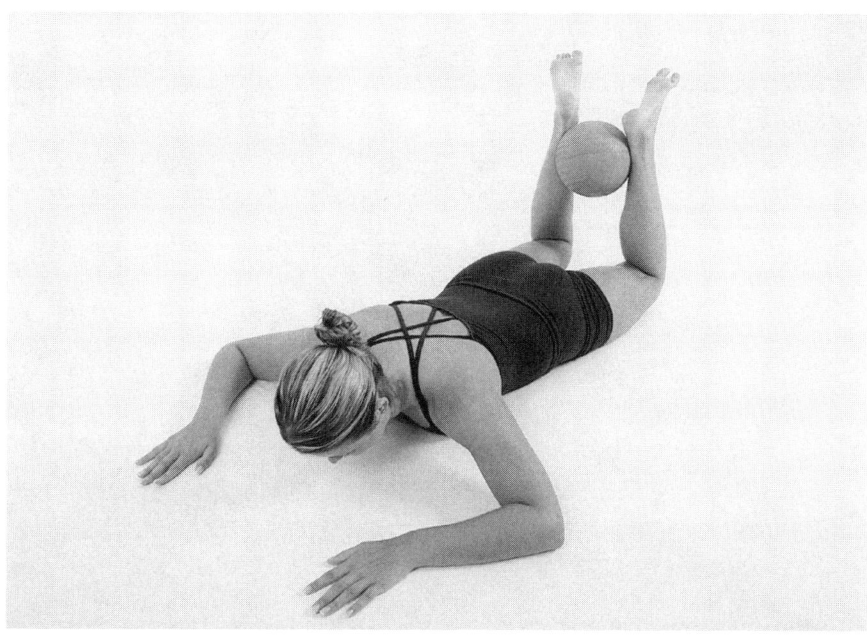

Photo 7.17
Back Leg Curl

Back Leg Curl

1. Lie on your stomach with your hands on the floor in front of you and the ball squeezed between your ankles.

2. Inhale as you raise your legs, and hold for 5 seconds.

3. Exhale as you lower your legs, and repeat.

For a Challenge

You can activate more of your lower back by raising your arms straight out in front of you or above your head when performing this exercise.

Standing Calf Raise with Dumbbell

1. Stand facing the wall, holding a dumbbell in your right hand, and place your left hand against the wall for support. (Keep your left knee slightly bent throughout the movement.)

2. Exhale and slowly rise onto your toes of your right foot, coming up as far as possible.

Photo 7.18
Standing Calf Raise with Dumbbell

3. Inhale as you slowly lower yourself to the starting position, and repeat.

4. After completing the sets, switch to the other foot and repeat.

LOWER-BACK WORKOUT

For these last exercises, you'll focus on the lower-back muscles. Place your legs shoulder-width apart. As you become stronger you can bring your legs together.

Hyperextension on the Floor

1. Lie facedown on the floor, keeping your neck in a neutral position, with your arms relaxed down by your sides.

2. Contract your right leg muscles and inhale as you slowly raise the leg.

Photo 7.19
Hyperextension on the Floor

3. Hold for 2 seconds at the top of the position, exhale as you slowly lower the leg, and repeat with the opposite leg.

4. Alternate legs for set repetitions—after completing one set with one leg, then switch to the other.

Key Points to Remember

- Hold in your stomach throughout the movement.
- Relax your upper back during the exercise, concentrating on the lower-back muscles and hips.
- Do not turn your hip over at the top of the movement, twisting your leg higher.
- Keep the leg straight.

One-Leg/One-Arm Raise

1. Begin in the same position as for the previous exercise (lying facedown), but place your left arm up above your head.

2. Inhale, and raise your right leg while simultaneously raising your left arm.

Photo 7.20
One-Leg/One-Arm Raise

3. Hold for 2 seconds, exhale as you lower your arm and leg with control, and repeat with the opposite arm and leg.

4. Alternate raising and lowering legs with opposite arms for set repetitions.

Two-Leg Raise

1. Start in the same position as in the previous exercise (lying facedown) but with arms down by your sides.

2. Inhale, and raise both legs at the same time, with your head kept down and lifting slightly off the floor.

3. Hold at the top of the movement for 2 seconds, exhale as you lower your legs, and repeat.

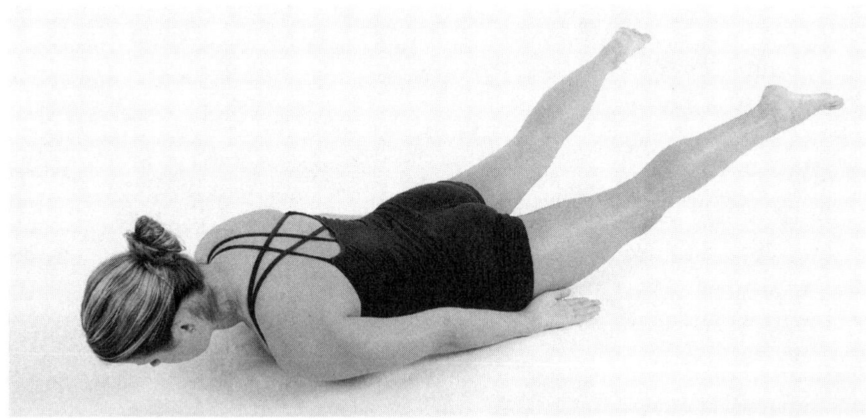

Photo 7.21
Two-Leg Raise

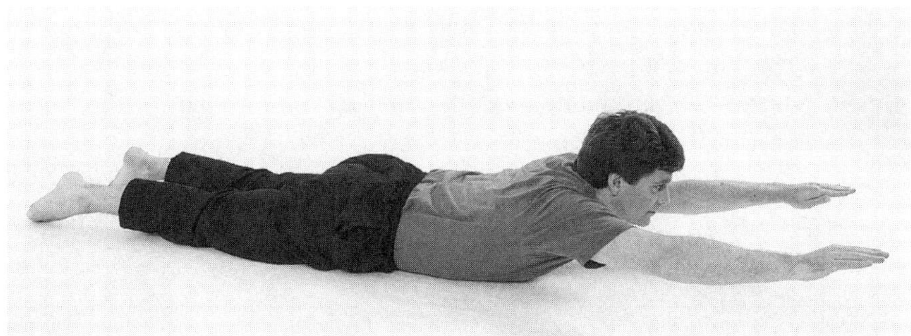

Photo 7.22
Two-Arm Raise

Two-Arm Raise

For this last exercise, remember to keep your glutes and legs relaxed throughout the movement to isolate the proper muscle groups.

1. Start in the same position as in the previous exercise (lying facedown) but with your arms outstretched in front.
2. Inhale, and raise both arms, with your head down and lifting slightly.
3. Hold for 2 seconds, exhale as you lower to the starting position, and repeat.

FITTING THE HOME WORKOUT INTO YOUR BUSY SCHEDULE

Joe, a 40-year-old doctor, came to me for help after injuring his back. He said he knew better than not to exercise on a regular basis and had tried the old tried-and-true back exercises but didn't feel any benefits from doing them.

I explained to him that he didn't need to join a gym just yet because he would only waste his money. Instead, I had him invest in a pair of dumbbells and a Swiss ball to use at home.

He began exercising at home in the mornings before going to work and used the wall stretches throughout the day in between seeing patients. He said he felt fewer aches and pains and now plans on adding a bench and more free weights in his home, because he wouldn't have the distractions or inconveniences a gym membership gave him in the past.

This whole-body regimen is well suited for most people and will prepare your body so you can perform daily activities—bending, lifting, walking, climbing stairs—without pain, injury, or discomfort. This part of the workout combined with the recommendations in the previous chapters will improve your posture and any muscle imbalances you may have. Now that you have a nice workout to start from out of your home, the next chapter offers more weight-training exercises that you can do at the gym and incorporate into the BackSmart program.

CHAPTER 8

WORKING OUT AT THE GYM

When you need more variety and motivation for working out, the gym is your environment. Your body tends to become accustomed to the exercises that you do for it. If you use the same exercise program at the same level of intensity, you'll eventually reach a sticking point, or your progress will come to a standstill.

I feel like a kid in a candy store when it comes to working out in the gym. There are so many machines from which to choose that I can do a completely different workout each time I go in. So, I do not understand why people go to the same machine every time they work out. I urge you to not let this happen to you. Instead, move around, explore different parts of the gym, and try out some new equipment. If you don't know how to use a piece of equipment, ask a staff member to show you. You should be getting your money's worth out of your membership.

One of the keys to a successful workout is to periodically vary the exercises you do each day as well as the way you do them. This way, as soon as your body starts adapting to what you are doing, you progressively intensify the program and avoid sticking points. The variety of equipment offered at the gym allows you to do just that.

WHAT TO WATCH OUT FOR AT THE GYM

While the gym offers a great deal of variety, there are a few important things you should keep in mind when choosing which equipment to use so that you have a safe and effective workout.

- **Be cautious when getting into and out of machines.** I have seen more people come through my office doors because they hurt themselves climbing into and out of the exercise machines than almost any other injury. This is most likely due to the fact that many of the new machines are ergonomically correct only if you are of standard height. Each equipment company has its own standards, and as we well know, people come in all shapes and sizes.

- **Avoid equipment that looks heavy and goes over you.** It's best not to push your luck or your spine's threshold; move on to a friendlier machine.

- **Be careful when strapping yourself into any machine that requires you to pull your body weight.** With some machines, the compression alone caused by the straps will put a significant load and strain on your lower spine.

- **Stay away from any machine that requires you to lock your legs into place and push backward (extension) for the lower back.** This type of machine should be banned, in my opinion, as too many people get hurt trying to force the weight back with a weak and inflexible spine.

- **People who suffer from back pain should avoid doing the barbell row—unlike the machine row, in which you are sitting and supporting your spine.** The barbell row forces you to either round your shoulders, arching the back, or bend too far forward while standing, which will cause stress on your disks. It's difficult to perform this exercise correctly, and when done improperly, it will cause more harm than good.

- **Avoid dumbbell flies and pec deck movements.** These exercises are commonly used by gym goers wanting to add shape to their chest muscles. Unfortunately, these movements are most often done incorrectly and with too much weight and cause too much stress at the shoulders and chest regions, resulting in tears and ruptures of the pectoral ligaments and tendons.

- **Finally, start off slowly.** Always ask for help if you are unfamiliar with the equipment.

ADDING HEALTHY TENSION WITH CABLES

This chapter will also demonstrate how to effectively isolate muscles by using cables during the movements. You will learn that free weights are not necessary to achieve that bodybuilder pump. If you don't belong to a gym that provides access to a cable machine, you can do these exercises at home using a resistance band. Place one side of the handle through a doorway, shut and lock the door to hold the band in place, and use the other side for resistance. You can also tie the band around the door handle—though this is not the best method.

Benefits of Working Out with Cables

The concept of cables or resistance bands is to accomplish fluidity and tension throughout the range of motion. The exercises in this section promote synchronization between muscle groups while simultaneously building strength and endurance. Emphasis is given to the legs and hips for stronger, shapelier muscles and increased endurance with fun, progressive exercises. You will also learn to enhance stamina while decreasing muscle tension and improving flexibility and balance throughout your body. I like to use these exercises regularly to keep the body working as a unit.

These movements place minimum stress on the joints while fatiguing out the muscles. I strongly advise against any pulsing or bouncing action during the repetitions, which can lead to jarring of the spinal nerves and disks.

Once you get used to the resistance and movement, you can change around the routine as you wish. I often recommend the cable exercises to patients who are not sure of themselves with free weights. You can interchange the movements for a complete workout without injuring your spine.

USING CABLES FOR A SOLID RESISTANCE-TRAINING WORKOUT

Alice, a 31-year-old graphic designer, spent many consecutive hours at the computer keyboard sitting in one position. She had developed carpal tunnel syndrome (wrist pain) and had difficulty lifting or turning objects without pain.

I started her out with the cable workout because it is continuous, without the jerky motion that sometimes occurs with lifting weights. Alice also couldn't use machine weights because the amount of pressure placed on her wrists was excessive.

The cable workout allowed her to have a complete resistance-training workout while strengthening her wrists at the same time. Within a few weeks, she was completing the cable workouts and adding the wall stretches to her routine. She said she has felt less pain as a result of using the BackSmart program.

Now that you know which machines to avoid and what to focus on, I encourage you to try these exercises and have a fun and challenging workout. Remember to do the BackSmart Daily Dozen (Chapter 4) before doing any resistance exercises, from free weights to machines. When learning each of the weight-training exercises in this chapter, use the following list as a guide for the number of sets and reps:

- **Beginner.** 2 sets of 10 to 12 repetitions.
- **Intermediate.** 3 sets of 10 to 12 repetitions.
- **Advanced.** 3 to 4 sets of 12 to 15 repetitions.

BACK AND LOWER-BACK WORKOUT

The first set of exercises will work the back muscles, with the last exercise focusing on strengthening the lower back.

Lat Pull-Down

Lat pull-down machines come in many varieties. The main thing to remember is that you are trying to pull yourself up with your entire upper body. The lat pull-down is similar to a chin-up, except you are able to build up to your body weight, or more, safely and without the fear of falling and injuring yourself in the process. Because this movement works the large back and shoulder muscles, you are able to handle a heavier weight. Start with 50 to 60 percent of your body weight, and add weight as you become stronger.

1. Place your hands shoulder-width apart and sit down.

2. Exhale as you pull the handles or bar down smoothly to the top of your chest, while rolling your shoulders back and squeezing your shoulder blades together.

3. Hold for 2 seconds and release.

4. Inhale as you slowly raise toward the top, and repeat.

Key Points to Remember

- Do not lock your legs in under the support. Locking your legs will not give you a greater stretch at the top of the movement and instead will pull on the psosas muscle group, which attaches to the back of your spine. This will cause a forced curve in your lower back.

- Do not pull the machine behind your head, as this will force your head forward, causing undue stress on your upper spine.

- Do not lean back, as this will cause undue stress on the lower back.

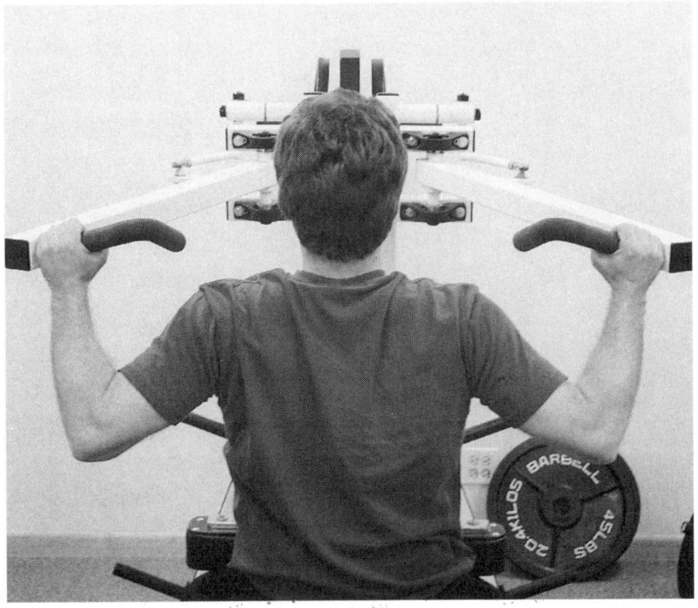

Photo 8.1
Lat Pull-Down

Machine Row

There are a few variations that can be done on the rowing machine nowadays, and all of them rely on your sitting on a seat or bench and leaning your chest against a support. Remember to sit up straight and keep your abdominal muscles pulled in during the exercise.

Many people think this machine is designed for an arm workout, when in fact it is not. When done correctly, this exercise uses your back muscles, because you are contracting them as you squeeze back.

1. Sit with your chest resting against the pad. Set the machine so that you are far enough away from the handles that you must stand up and reach them before sitting down.

2. Exhale, and pull the handles back, keeping your shoulders down. (Squeeze your shoulder blades as if you are holding something between them.)

3. Hold for 2 seconds, inhale as you return to the starting position (without releasing the tension), and repeat.

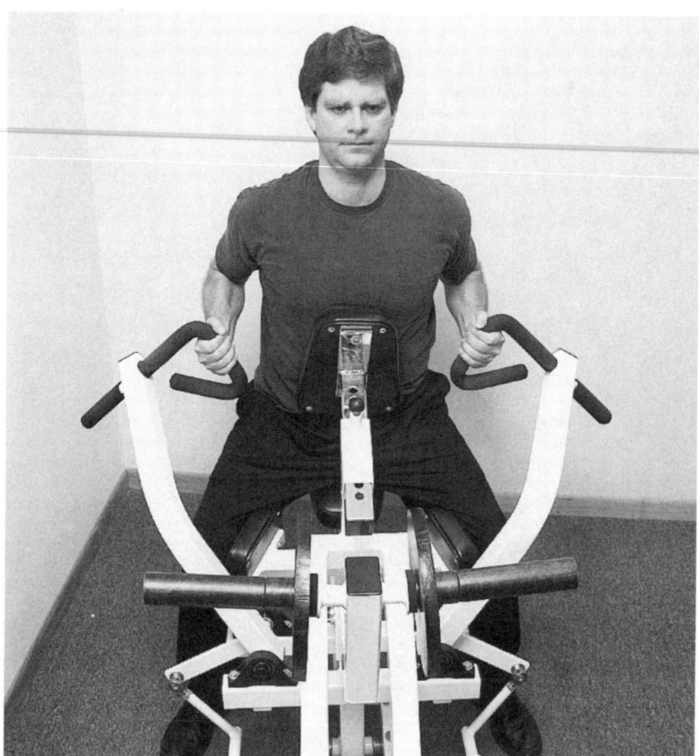

Photo 8.2
Machine Row

Key Points to Remember

- Your lower chest should be touching the upper part of the bench pad only at the end of the contraction, and you should be arching your back slightly at peak contraction.

- Do not sit too close to the weight stack, as doing so will not give you the complete stretch or contraction needed for muscle stimulation.

- Do not sit too low in the seat. Rowing behind the bench will give you a good posterior deltoid workout only and not the back workout that is intended with this exercise.

Kneeling Cable Lateral Pull-Down

You will feel this next exercise behind your shoulders and in the muscles of your back.

1. Holding a cable in each hand, kneel facing the wall, about three to four feet away.

2. Beginning at head height with your arms shoulder-width apart, exhale as you slowly lower your straightened arms toward your thighs.

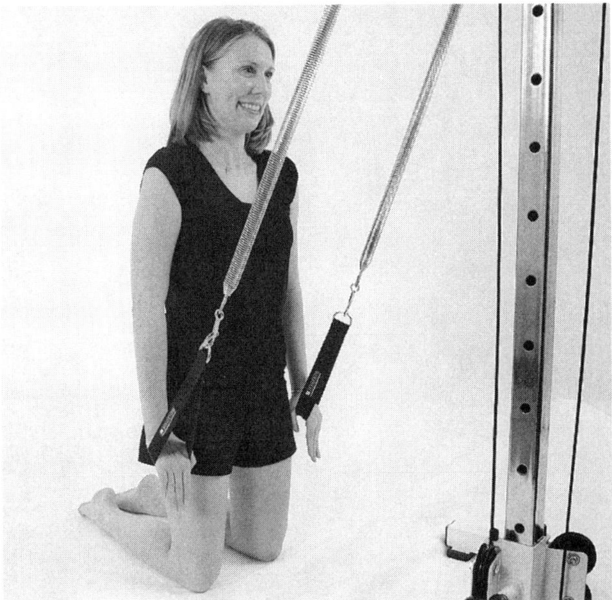

Photo 8.3
Kneeling Cable Lateral Pull-Down

3. Hold for 2 seconds, inhale as you return to the starting position, and repeat.

For a Challenge

To engage your triceps and shoulder muscles, in step 2, bring your arms past your waist behind you as far as you can.

Back Kick

This next exercise uses your body weight, and you can do it with the hyperextension machine or, if you're at home, while holding the back of a stable chair.

1. Face the hyperextension machine (or chair back), with your hands either resting on top or holding the handles. Your feet should be shoulder-width apart.

Photos 8.4, 8.5 Back Kick

2. Raise your right knee toward your chest and hold for 2 seconds.

3. Exhale as you drop the leg backward and straighten it waist high.

4. Inhale as you return your leg up to your chest, and hold for 2 seconds.

5. Slowly lower your leg until your toes touch the floor, and repeat.

6. After 2 to 4 sets of 10 to 15 repetitions, repeat the exercise with the opposite leg.

BICEPS WORKOUT

The next set of exercises will focus primarily on the biceps muscles. You'll be using a workout bench and weights.

Preacher Bench Curl with Dumbbell

For this exercise, you'll be working one arm at a time. Make sure to sit so that your lower chest is higher than the top of the bench. Many people make the mistake of sitting too low and thus stressing the tendons and ligaments of the biceps into the deltoid joint, causing tears and strains that are easily prevented by raising the seat.

1. Start with your chest against the bench and your arm extended over the bench. (This puts the arms at an angle, which transfers additional stress to the lower area of the muscle.)

2. Pick up the dumbbell with an underhand grip.

3. Holding the dumbbell steady, inhale as you curl up the weight.

4. Exhale and lower your arm again to a full extension, resisting the weight on the way down.

5. After completing your repetitions with one arm, repeat the exercise with the other arm.

Photo 8.6
Preacher Bench Curl
with Dumbbell

Bench Curls on an Incline

Performing this next movement on the incline bench will reduce the amount of secondary muscles involved in curling the weight, causing more of an isolation to the biceps group.

1. With a dumbbell in each hand, straddle the incline bench and lower yourself onto it facedown. Rest your chest on the bench, with your feet firmly planted on the floor.

2. Inhale, and slowly curl your arms up toward your shoulders.

3. Exhale as you lower the weights, and repeat.

Photo 8.7
Bench Curls on an Incline

Cable Curls

1. Stand in front of the machine, with your feet shoulder-width apart. Grasp the handles with your palms up and resting on your thighs.

2. Slowly walk back one to two feet so there is tension in your arms, holding the weight at the starting position.

3. Inhale as you slowly curl up toward your shoulders, squeezing your biceps hard at the top.

4. Exhale as you slowly lower your arms, and repeat.

BackSmart Alternative

If you suffer from back pain, you can lie on the floor and perform the same exercise without stressing your back.

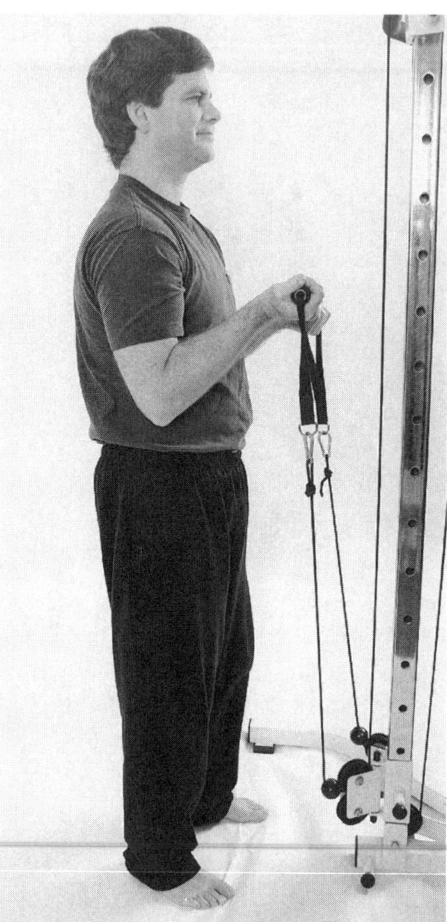

Photo 8.8
Cable Curls

SHOULDER WORKOUT

This next set of exercises will give your shoulders a nice workout. You'll be using the incline bench and a set of dumbbells. These exercises demonstrate some examples of how you can incorporate basic weight training into your workout routine at the gym by using the incline bench so that your back is not compromised and you still have an effective workout.

Lying Side Dumbbell Lateral

1. Sit sideways on the incline board and lie on your left side. Hold on to the top of the board with your left hand.

Photo 8.9
Lying Side Dumbbell Lateral

2. Hold a dumbbell in your right hand, with a slight bend at the elbow, and raise your arm so that it is parallel to the side of your face.

3. Exhale as you lower the weight until it is almost touching the bench.

4. Inhale as you raise the dumbbell near the top of the movement. (Twist your hand slightly while lifting, turning the thumb down to further contract the rear deltoid.)

5. After completing the reps, switch arms and repeat the exercise on the other side.

Front Raise

1. Sit with your back against the incline bench and your feet firmly on the floor. Hold a dumbbell in each hand with the top of your hands facing forward. Your feet should be shoulder-width apart.

2. With a slight bend at the elbow, inhale as you raise one dumbbell to face height.

3. Hold for 2 seconds, exhale as you slowly lower the weight to the starting position, and repeat with the other arm.

4. Continue alternating arms to complete the sets until you complete the same number of repetitions with each arm to finish one set.

Photo 8.10
Front Raise

Military Press

This next exercise is used to strengthen your shoulder region and upper-neck muscles. This is a good compounded movement in which you can work many muscles at once without concentrating on balancing any weights in the process, allowing you to focus on the muscles and your posture.

1. Sit all the way back in the machine, flattening your lower back and the back of your head against the seat. (Tilt your chin down slightly throughout the pressing movement.)

2. Grasp the bar at shoulder level, and exhale while pressing upward until your arms are locked out.

3. Inhale as you slowly lower the weight to the starting position (going through the longest range of motion possible), and repeat.

Key Points to Remember

Keeping these following points in mind will help you avoid the many mistakes that can occur during this exercise that can cause you a lot of pain down the road.

- Do not look up at the ceiling or toward the side when pressing up. Doing so can cause nerve root damage in the neck region.

- Keep your entire back and head against the seat throughout the movement.

Photo 8.11
Military Press

- Breathe continuously; do not hold your breath during any part of the movement.

- Keep your feet flat on the floor at all times.

Cable Lateral Raise

1. Stand with your left side toward the machine, holding the cable handle in your right hand.

2. Walk out two to three feet, maintaining the tension in the cable. Stand with your feet shoulder-width apart and knees bent slightly.

3. Looking straight ahead, exhale as you pull the cable up toward head height.

4. Inhale as you lower the handle in a slow arc in front of your body, and repeat with the opposite side after completing one set.

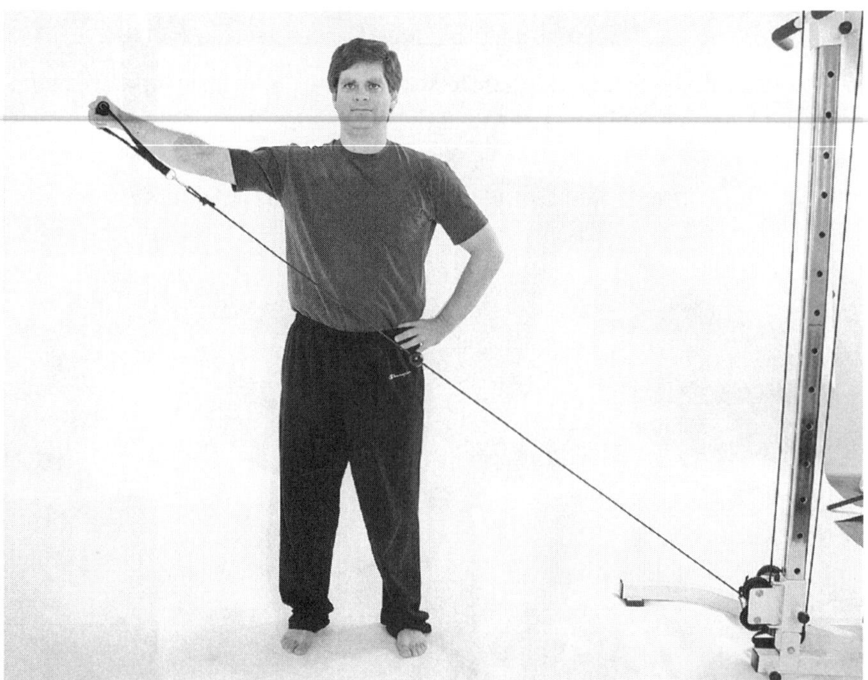

Photo 8.12
Cable Lateral Raise

For a Challenge
This exercise can be done with the cable behind you for a different feel on the deltoid muscle group; you can also do alternate sets of each variation.

TRICEPS WORKOUT

The next set of exercises targets the triceps muscles and requires use of the cable machine. Using the cable permits continuous tension on the muscles and a deep stretch at the bottom of the movement.

Triceps Cable Push-Down

1. Stand in front of the cable machine and grasp the handle (attached to a pulley above you) with an overhead grip. Your hands should be about 10 inches apart, with your elbows tucked in close to your body and remaining stationary.

2. Exhale as you press the bar down as far as possible, locking out your arms and feeling the triceps contract fully.

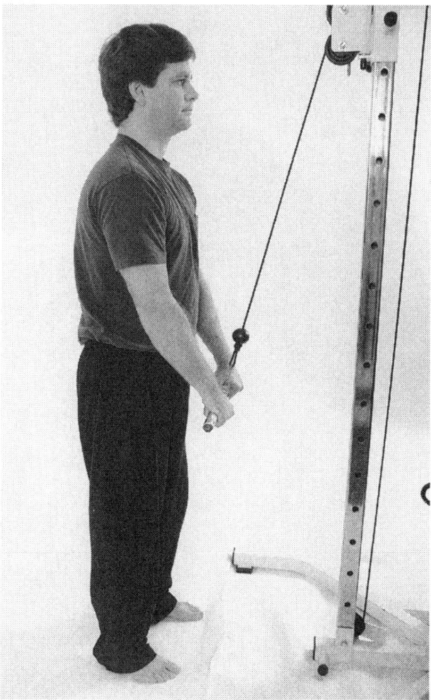

Photo 8.13
Triceps Cable
Push-Down

3. Inhale as you release the bar as high as possible without moving your elbows, return to the starting position, and repeat.

Key Points to Remember

- Concentrate on keeping your elbows stationary at your sides and your wrists locked throughout the movement.
- Do not raise and lower your shoulders during the movement.
- Keep your whole body steady. Don't lean forward to press down with your body weight.

Seated Cable Extension

1. Sit on a Swiss ball with your back to the machine, and grasp the handle with one hand.

Photo 8.14
Seated Cable Extension

2. Inhale as you press the handle above and slightly forward from your head, extending your arm completely.

3. Exhale as you lower behind your head, and repeat.

One-Arm Overhead Cable Extension

1. Stand facing away from the cable machine and grasp the handle above your head with one hand.

2. Take two or three steps forward, keeping your elbow bent and your hand level with your face.

3. Exhale as you push out and extend the arm forward.

4. Inhale as you bend your arm and return the handle to the height of your face.

5. After completing the sets, repeat the exercise with the other arm.

Photo 8.15
One-Arm Overhead
Cable Extension

CHEST WORKOUT

The next set of exercises will work the chest muscles before you move on to exercises that work the lower body.

Incline Chest Press

1. Lie back on the incline press bench, with your lower back flat against the bench throughout the movement.

2. Reach up and grasp the handles with a medium-wide grip.

3. Lift the handles off the rack and hold it straight overhead, with your arms locked.

4. Inhale as you lower toward your upper chest, and stop for a moment.

5. Exhale as you press back up to the starting position, and repeat.

Photo 8.16
Incline Chest Press

Dumbbell Bench Press

For this next exercise, you will have to use lighter dumbbells than are normal for you, for balance. Your feet will remain up on the bench instead of on the floor, to avoid excessive stress and arching of the lower back.

1. Lie on your back on the bench, with your knees bent and your feet on the bench.

2. Hold a dumbbell in each hand and raise the weights straight up overhead, with your palms facing forward.

3. Inhale as you lower the weights toward your chest, concentrating on keeping them fully balanced and under control. Lower them as far as you can, feeling a complete stretch in the chest muscles.

4. Exhale as you press the weights back up and lock your arms straight overhead.

5. Touch the dumbbells at the top of the movement, causing a contraction in the chest muscle groups; lower the weights and repeat.

Photos 8.17, 8.18 Dumbbell Bench Press

Key Points to Remember

- Keep your lower back flat throughout the exercise.
- Don't let your ego get the best of you; using too much weight or getting sloppy with your form will cause you injuries.

Dip Between Benches

The dipping movement is a good all-around exercise for the arms and lower-chest region.

1. Sit on the workout bench with a chair in front of you. Leaning forward slightly will activate more of the chest muscles.
2. Put your feet up on the chair, and hold yourself at arms' length above the bench.
3. Inhale as you slowly lower yourself as far as you can.
4. From the bottom, exhale as you press back up to the starting position, tensing your chest muscles at the top; repeat.

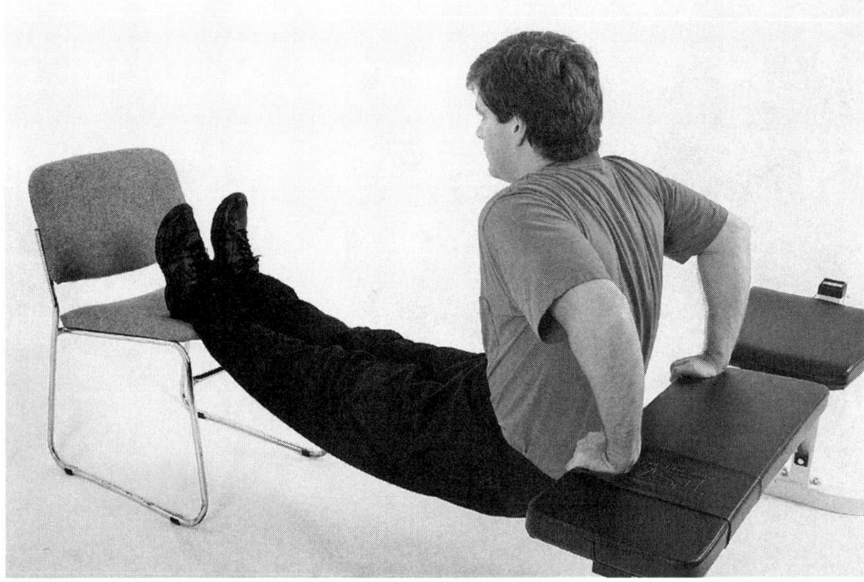

Photo 8.19
Dip Between Benches

For a Challenge

To add intensity to the movement, you can place weights on your lap or around your waist.

Weight Push-Up

This is a great exercise to do at the end of your workout. Follow the instructions for basic push-ups in the home workout in Chapter 7 for proper form, only this time, place a 25-pound or 45-pound plate on your upper back (be sure to have a spotter!) and rep out as many push-ups as you can. This will build an impressive amount of endurance.

LEG WORKOUT

These last exercises work the lower half of the body, using machines that concentrate on the legs.

Leg Extension

Using the leg extension machine is an effective means of working the front of your leg without straining your back. Because you are sitting with your back supported, you stabilize your spine and prevent injuries from occurring—unlike with the weighted squat, which places considerable stress on your disks. When working on this machine, you should use a weight that is light enough to allow a complete range of motion.

1. Sit at the machine with your legs shoulder-width apart, and hook your ankles behind the pad so that it is resting on top of your ankles.

2. Exhale as you straighten your legs and lift the weight as high as possible.

3. Hold for 2 seconds, inhale as you slowly lower to the starting position, and repeat.

Key Points to Remember

- Make sure you always extend your legs fully enough.

- Do not let your hips come off the seat during the movement; remain sitting flat.

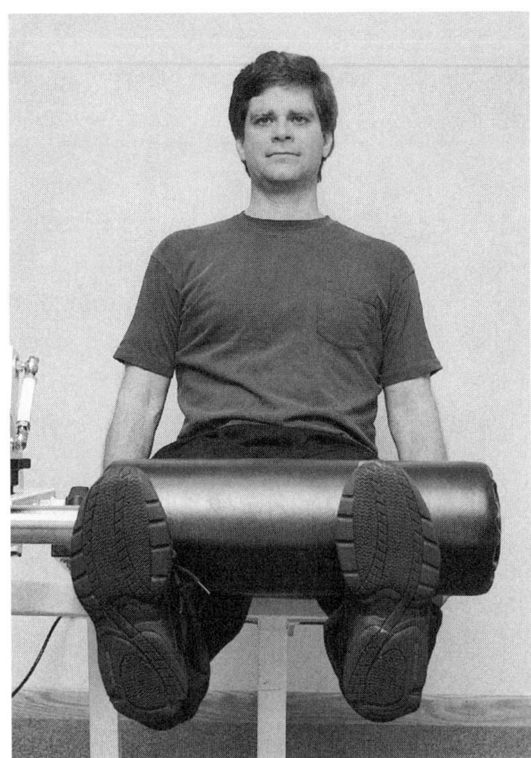

Photo 8.20
Leg Extension

- If your knees are sore or you have had injuries to your knee region, do the exercise with as much range of motion as possible without locking out at the top of the movement.

Leg Curls

The leg curl machine will add a new dimension to your workouts by isolating the back of your hamstrings right above your knees and your hip muscles. Remember not to arch your back when performing this movement, and try not to raise your hips off the machine during the contraction phase. This exercise should be done strictly and through the fullest range of motion possible.

1. Lie facedown on the bench and hook your heels under the pad.

2. Stretch your legs out straight, and hold on to the handles or the bench itself to keep yourself from lifting up off the bench.

Photo 8.21
Leg Curls

3. Keeping flat on the bench, inhale as you curl your legs up as far as possible, until they are fully contracted.

4. Hold for 2 seconds, release, and exhale as you slowly lower back to the starting position and repeat.

Single-Leg Cable

Cables are a great way to work your legs with fluid movement and constant tension. Your legs will feel pumped up from being worked this way. Try to concentrate on squeezing and holding the positions for the desired effect. You can use springs or bands for resistance.

1. Lie on your back on the floor, with the straps around your feet at the instep and with one leg raised. Keep your lower back flat on the floor and your arms down by your sides.

2. Begin to squeeze the front of your legs as you exhale and slowly lower the raised leg to the floor.

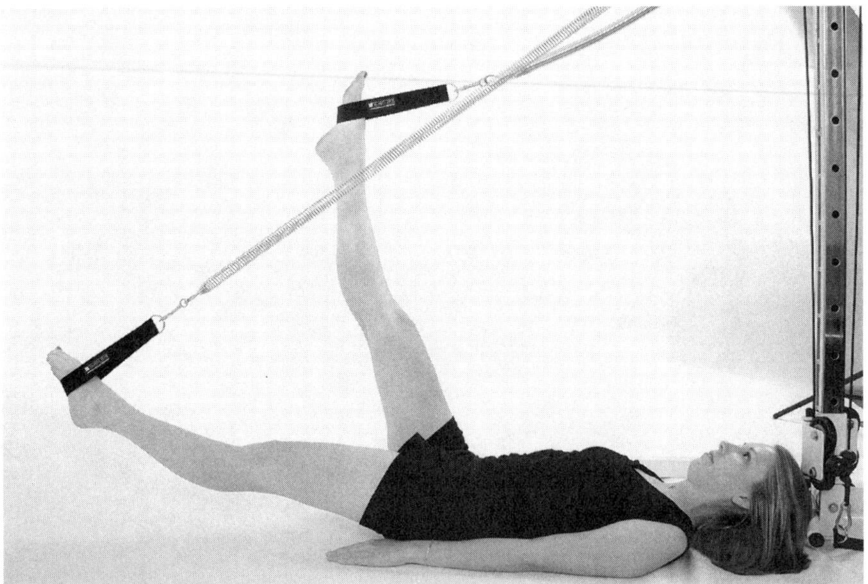

Photo 8.22
Single-Leg Cable

3. Hold at the bottom for 2 seconds, inhale as you return your leg to the raised starting position, and repeat with the opposite leg.

4. Complete the sets by alternating legs.

Cable Squat

1. Face the wall, standing about three to five feet away. Your feet should be shoulder-width apart and flat on the floor throughout the exercise. Hold the cables in both hands.

2. Slowly pull the cables in at shoulder height toward your chest. Squeeze your shoulder blades back tightly, feeling your back muscles work against the resistance, as you pull your stomach muscles and hold them tight throughout the movement.

3. Exhale as you slowly squat until your thighs are parallel to the floor (or farther down, depending on your flexibility).

4. Hold for 2 seconds, inhale as you rise to the starting position, and immediately repeat.

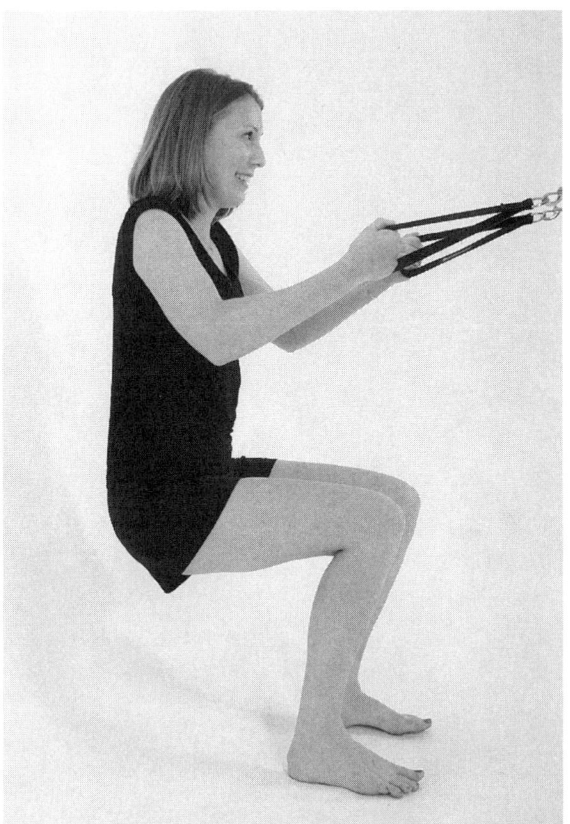

Photo 8.23
Cable Squat

One-Leg Cable Squat

This more challenging squatting exercise will help you develop superior strength in your legs and hips as well as balance.

1. Get into the same position as for the cable squat (facing the wall with your feet shoulder-width apart and holding the straps in both hands).

2. Exhale as you slowly lean back while bending your knees, and lift your left foot off the floor. (Drop your hips.)

3. Inhale as you slowly return to the starting position, and repeat. Complete one set of reps on one side before switching to the opposite leg.

Photo 8.24
One-Leg Cable Squat

GETTING OUT OF A FAMILIAR RUT

Jill, a 30-year-old marketing consultant, always worked out in gyms when she was traveling. She fell into a rut, doing the same exercises every time. She said she tried changing the order of her exercises but was dissatisfied with her results.

In reviewing Jill's workouts on-site, I noticed that she started off doing cardio and then would use all the weight-training equipment on the right-hand side of the gym and finally move her way back to the locker area to finish her workout. She said she had never realized that she was doing that—even when she changed her workouts.

I started Jill with the intermediate level of the BackSmart program, which took her through the sequence of exercises designed to give her maximum results while cross-training in the gym. She told me, "I could really feel the difference after my first workout. I was all over the gym, using the walls and machines in an order that made me feel my muscles working."

Like Jill, you can easily fall into a familiar routine that you do every time you go to the gym. By incorporating the BackSmart gym workout into your exercise program, you'll be able to find the challenges and variety that you need to get stronger and stay motivated as you work toward your fitness goals.

PART 3

Putting It All Together: The BackSmart Fitness Program

CHAPTER 9

CREATING YOUR BACKSMART WORKOUT

After you have learned how to perform the individual exercises in Part 2, you can apply the information in this chapter to choose a workout plan that best suits you, based on your age and fitness level. In addition, I have included suggestions for routines designed to achieve specific goals such as losing weight, toning your midsection, getting fit after having a baby, and exercising safely with arthritic pain or other conditions. The examples provided are based on my experiences with patients of all ages and fitness levels. You can mix and match the programs if you like, or simply begin with the basic level and progress to the intermediate level and, finally, the advanced program.

CHOOSING YOUR LEVEL OF TRAINING

Each of the following three programs is geared to a specific level of progress. Choose your level—beginner, intermediate, or advanced—according to what your goals are and how much time you want to spend exercising each day. The levels differ in how many sets are done and the number of repetitions performed during each set. Also, as you progress to the next higher level, the stretches are held for a longer time. Each of these levels is different from the others, and each succeeding one is progressively more challenging.

When following any of these programs, remember to focus on feeling the muscles working and on connecting your mind with the movements. As you become more comfortable with the exercises, review the key points discussed in Chapter 3, which will help keep you on course on your road to success.

Basic Program

The basic level is a good one to choose if you haven't done much exercise. It is perfect for people who don't have a lot of time to exercise each day (no more than 20 to 30 minutes at a time). It's also good for those who just want to stay trim and well toned.

Two sets of each weight-training exercise is a great starting point for most people; you can add repetitions per set before adding another set, or the other way around if you like. How long you rest between sets at the beginning is determined by how long it takes for your breathing to return to normal, which is usually within 30 seconds to a minute, depending on your current state of fitness. Do not get caught up in watching the time; if you are short of breath, take a longer break between sets.

Refer to the breathing exercises in Chapter 3, and make them a part of your training from day one. This will give you more energy and will speed your recuperation time. The emphasis in this first level of training is on performing all exercises correctly.

Weeks 1–4

Do the BackSmart Daily Dozen stretches in the morning, at lunchtime, or in the evening 5 to 7 days per week.

BackSmart Pilates

Do a modified Pilates and ab workout (in the order prescribed) at lunchtime or in the evening every other day, 3 to 5 days per week.

Hundreds	2 sets of 25 to 50 repetitions
Corkscrews	2 sets of 10 to 25 repetitions
Scissors	2 sets of 10 to 25 repetitions
Double Leg Stretches	2 sets of 10 to 25 repetitions

Abs

Crunches—Hands on Knees	2 sets of 10 to 25 repetitions
Reverse Crunches	2 sets of 10 to 25 repetitions

Aerobics

Walk 1 to 2 miles, or for 20 to 30 minutes, 4 to 7 days per week.

Weekly Plan

	Mon	Tues	Wed	Thur	Fri	Sat	Sun
Stretching	X	X	X	X	X		
BackSmart Pilates	X		X		X		
Abs	X		X		X		
Aerobics	X	X	X	X	X		

Weeks 5–9

Do the BackSmart Daily Dozen stretches in the morning, at lunchtime, and in the evening 5 to 7 days per week. Perform the wall stretches along with your workouts, and do the specified shower stretches in Chapter 4 for an added cooldown.

BackSmart Pilates

Do these in the morning or evening every other day, 3 or 4 days per week.

Hundreds	3 to 4 sets of 25 to 40 repetitions
Corkscrews	3 to 4 sets of 10 to 25 repetitions
Scissors	3 to 4 sets of 10 to 25 repetitions
Double Leg Stretches	3 to 4 sets of 10 to 25 repetitions

Weights

Add dumbbells and complete this sequence of exercises for a full-body workout 2 to 4 times per week, every other day.

Biceps

Wall/Arm Curls	2 to 3 sets of 10 to 20 repetitions

Back

Dumbbell Pull-Overs	2 to 4 sets of 10 to 15 repetitions
Lat Pull-Downs	2 to 4 sets of 10 to 15 repetitions

Lower Back

Hyperextensions on the Floor	2 sets of 10 to 15 repetitions
One-Leg/One-Arm Raises	2 sets of 10 to 15 repetitions

Shoulder

Dumbbell Presses Against the Wall	3 to 4 sets of 10 to 15 repetitions
Lateral Raises	3 to 4 sets of 10 to 15 repetitions

Triceps

Dumbbell Kickbacks	3 to 4 sets of 10 to 15 repetitions

Chest

Dumbbell Bench Presses	4 to 5 sets of 10 to 15 repetitions
Incline Chest Presses	4 to 5 sets of 10 to 15 repetitions

Leg

Karate Front Stances	2 to 3 sets of 10 to 15 repetitions
Two-Leg Lifts with Ball Between Knees	2 sets of 10 to 20 repetitions

Abdominal Workout

Do the following ab workout 3 or 4 times per week every other day.

Day 1

Seated Knee-Ups	2 to 3 sets of 10 to 25 repetitions
Hip Raises	2 to 3 sets of 10 to 25 repetitions
Toe-Touch Crunches with a Twist	2 to 3 sets of 10 to 25 repetitions
Crunches—Butterfly Position	2 to 3 sets of 10 to 25 repetitions

Day 2

Bicycles	2 to 3 sets of 10 to 25 repetitions
Knees-to-Elbows Side Leg Lifts	2 to 3 sets of 10 to 25 repetitions

Day 3

Froggies	2 to 3 sets of 10 to 25 repetitions
Crunches—Hands on Knees	2 to 3 sets of 10 to 25 repetitions
Reverse Crunches	2 to 3 sets of 10 to 25 repetitions
Crunches—Butterfly Position	2 to 3 sets of 10 to 25 repetitions

Swiss Ball Workout

Add Swiss ball exercises this month, improving balance and coordination, 2 times per week.

Swiss Ball Crunches	2 to 3 sets of 10 to 25 repetitions
Single-Hamstring Lifts	2 to 3 sets of 10 to 25 repetitions

Balance Drills

Add balance drills 2 times per week.

Standing Asleep — 2 to 3 sets of 30 seconds to 1 minute

Aerobics

Increase the duration of walking to 30 to 45 minutes 4 to 7 days per week, or continue the same amount of time but walk more frequently.

Weekly Plan

	Mon	Tues	Wed	Thur	Fri	Sat	Sun
Stretching	X	X	X	X	X	X	X
BackSmart Pilates	X	X			X		X
Weights	X	X			X	X	
Cable	X		X				
Aerobics	X	X	X	X	X	X	X
Abs	X	X		X	X		
Ball			X		X		
Balance Drills			X		X		

Try to add one sport into your weekly schedule. You should feel more confident at this stage. You will still feel sore after exercising, but you should strive to increase the number of reps and sets progressively each week.

Intermediate Program

The intermediate-level program is for those who want to increase their muscular strength and endurance and who are more experienced with exercising and weight training. It can also be used by those who have just completed the first six weeks of the basic program and wish to gain strength to develop a harder, firmer look to the body. This program emphasizes exercises in the exact areas intended. Each workout at this level takes slightly longer to complete than those in the basic program.

Always increase the amount of weight used at the intermediate level, even if you have to do fewer repetitions at the beginning. Another great way to enhance your workouts at this level is to incorporate the wall stretches or the BackSmart Daily Dozen stretches into your exercises by immediately following a set of exercises with a stretch, and then take a short rest to allow your breathing rate to return to normal. Perform the next sets in the same manner—following the completed reps with a stretch and then a rest period.

Weeks 10–15

Do the BackSmart Daily Dozen stretches two times a day—in the morning and evening—5 to 7 days per week. Perform the prescribed shower stretches from Chapter 4 in the morning, and incorporate the wall stretches daily into your workout routine.

Advanced Ladder/Stair Stretches

Complete these in the evening, 5 to 7 days per week.

Front Leg Raises	2 sets of 10 to 20 repetitions
Side Leg Lifts	2 sets of 10 to 20 repetitions

BackSmart Pilates

Do these exercises 4 to 5 times a week in the morning or evening.

Hundreds	3 to 4 sets of 25 to 50 repetitions
Corkscrews	3 to 4 sets of 10 to 25 repetitions
Scissors	3 to 4 sets of 10 to 25 repetitions
Double Leg Stretches	3 to 4 sets of 10 to 25 repetitions
Teasers	2 sets of 10 to 25 repetitions
Seals	2 sets of 10 repetitions
Leg Raises	2 to 3 sets of 10 to 25 repetitions

Weights

Do these 3 times per week, adding machine workouts, cable workouts, or home workouts. Gradually increase to 4 to 5 sets per body part, more for the larger groups. Choose 2 to 4 movements for one workout day, and then for the next workout, change the order of exercises or change to different movements. Always keep your muscles guessing.

Biceps

Wall/Arm Curls	2 to 4 sets of 10 to 20 repetitions
One-Arm Curls Holding the Wall	2 to 4 sets of 10 to 20 repetitions
Cable Curls	2 to 4 sets of 10 to 20 repetitions

Back

Dumbbell Pull-Overs	2 to 4 sets of 10 to 20 repetitions
Lat Pull-Downs	2 to 5 sets of 10 to 20 repetitions
Dumbbell Rows	2 to 4 sets of 10 to 20 repetitions

Lower Back

Hyperextensions on the Floor	2 to 3 sets of 10 to 20 repetitions
One-Leg/One-Arm Raises	2 to 3 sets of 10 to 20 repetitions
Two-Leg Raises	2 to 3 sets of 10 to 20 repetitions
Two-Arm Raises	2 to 3 sets of 10 to 20 repetitions

Shoulder

Dumbbell Presses Against the Wall	3 to 4 sets of 10 to 15 repetitions
Lateral Raises	3 to 4 sets of 10 to 15 repetitions
Bent-Over Lateral Raises	3 to 4 sets of 10 to 15 repetitions

Triceps

Dumbbell Kickbacks	3 to 4 sets of 10 to 15 repetitions
Bench or Stair Push-Ups	2 to 3 sets of 10 to 15 repetitions

Chest

Dumbbell Bench Presses	3 to 4 sets of 10 to 15 repetitions
Incline Chest Presses	3 to 5 sets of 10 to 15 repetitions
Dips Between Benches	3 to 4 sets of 10 to 15 repetitions

Leg

Karate Front Stances	2 to 4 sets of 10 to 15 repetitions
Back Leg Curls	2 to 4 sets of 10 to 15 repetitions
Leg Extensions	2 to 4 sets of 10 to 15 repetitions
Standing Calf Raises with Dumbbell	2 to 3 sets of 10 to 15 repetitions

Cable Workout

Do these 2 to 3 times per week.

Cable Squats	2 to 4 sets of 10 to 25 repetitions
One-Leg Cable Squats	2 to 3 sets of 10 to 25 repetitions
Single-Leg Cables	2 to 3 sets of 10 to 25 repetitions
Triceps Cable Push-Downs	2 to 4 sets of 10 to 25 repetitions

Abdominal Workout

Do these 4 to 6 days per week.

Day 1

Crunches—Hands on Knees	2 to 3 sets of 10 to 25 repetitions
Reverse Crunches	2 to 3 sets of 10 to 25 repetitions
Crunches—Butterfly Position	2 to 3 sets of 10 to 25 repetitions

Day 2

Seated Knee-Ups	2 to 3 sets of 10 to 25 repetitions
Hip Raises	2 to 3 sets of 10 to 25 repetitions
Toe-Touch Crunches with a Twist	2 to 3 sets of 10 to 25 repetitions

Day 3

Reverse Crunches	2 to 3 sets of 10 to 15 repetitions
Oblique Side Crunches	2 to 3 sets of 10 to 25 repetitions
Knees-to-Elbows Side Leg Lifts	2 to 3 sets of 10 to 25 repetitions

Day 4

Froggies	2 to 3 sets of 10 to 25 repetitions
Leg Raises on Your Elbows	2 to 3 sets of 10 to 25 repetitions

Day 5

Medicine Ball Crunches in Front	2 to 3 sets of 10 to 25 repetitions
Bicycles	2 to 3 sets of 10 to 25 repetitions
V Sit-Ups Against the Wall	2 to 3 sets of 10 to 25 repetitions

Swiss Ball Workout

Add Swiss ball exercises this month, improving balance and coordination, 2 to 3 times per week.

Swiss Ball Crunches	2 to 3 sets of 10 to 25 repetitions
Single-Hamstring Lifts	2 to 3 sets of 10 to 25 repetitions
Side-Lying Airplane Rolls	2 to 3 sets of 10 to 25 repetitions

Balance Drills

Add balance drills 2 to 3 times per week.

Standing Asleep	2 to 3 sets of 30 seconds to 1 minute
Front Kicks	2 to 3 sets of 6 to 12 repetitions
Exercise Back Kicks	2 to 3 sets of 6 to 12 repetitions

Aerobics

Increase the amount of time or speed, walking 5 to 7 days per week. Add biking or cross-training to your routine 1 to 2 times per week, substituting for a walking day.

Weekly Plan

	Mon	Tues	Wed	Thur	Fri	Sat	Sun
Stretching	X	X	X	X	X	X	X
BackSmart Pilates	X	X	X		X		
Weights	X		X		X		
Cable	X		X		X		
Abs	X	X	X	X	X	X	
Aerobics	X	X	X	X	X	X	X
Ball	X			X	X		
Balance Drills	X		X		X		

Advanced Program

The advanced program is for people who have more experience with exercise—at least six months of weight training—and have been exercising for at least one to three hours a week and want to get maximum results. It is also for people who have just completed the intermediate level and are ready to move up. This advanced level is made up of three sets of each weight-training exercise, followed by wall stretches or the BackSmart Daily Dozen stretches.

At the advanced level, try to rest as little as possible between sets. Do not worry too much about increasing the weight on every set. Your main concern is moving through your workout without wasting time. This kind of training promotes excellent muscle tone and definition.

Weeks 16–20

Do the BackSmart Daily Dozen Stretches twice a day—in the morning and evening. Incorporate the wall stretches daily into your workout routine. End your routine with the shower stretches.

Advanced Stretches

Add these advanced stretches on stairs or a ladder 2 to 3 days per week.

Front Leg Raises	2 sets of 10 to 20 repetitions
Bent-Knee Stretches	2 sets of 10 to 20 repetitions
Side-Kick Stretches	2 sets of 10 to 20 repetitions
Standing Bent-Leg Twists	2 sets of 10 to 20 repetitions

BackSmart Pilates Workout

Complete the following exercises 4 times a week in the morning or evening every other day.

Hundreds	3 to 4 sets of 25 to 50 repetitions
Corkscrews	3 to 4 sets of 10 to 25 repetitions
Scissors	3 to 4 sets of 10 to 25 repetitions
Double Leg Stretches	3 to 4 sets of 10 to 25 repetitions
Teasers	3 to 4 sets of 10 to 25 repetitions
Seals	3 to 4 sets of 10 to 25 repetitions
Hip Circles	2 sets of 10 to 25 repetitions
Jackknives	2 sets of 10 to 25 repetitions
Single Straight Legs	2 sets of 10 to 25 repetitions

Weights

Do a weight-training workout 4 times per week with machines, cables, or home equipment. Gradually do 4 to 5 sets per body part, more for the larger groups. Choose 3 to 5 movements for one workout day, and then for the next workout, change the order of exercises or change to different movements. Always keep your muscles guessing. Alternate weights and cable workouts.

Biceps

Wall/Arm Curls	2 to 4 sets of 10 to 20 repetitions
Cable Curls	2 to 4 sets of 10 to 20 repetitions
Preacher Bench Curls with Dumbbell	2 to 4 sets of 10 to 15 repetitions
Bench Curls on an Incline	2 to 3 sets of 10 to 15 repetitions

Back

Dumbbell Pull-Overs	2 to 4 sets of 10 to 20 repetitions
Lat Pull-Downs	2 to 5 sets of 10 to 20 repetitions

Machine Rows	3 to 5 sets of 10 to 20 repetitions
Dumbbell Rows	2 to 3 sets of 10 to 15 repetitions

Lower Back

Hyperextensions on the Floor	2 to 3 sets of 10 to 20 repetitions
One-Leg/One-Arm Raises	2 to 3 sets of 10 to 20 repetitions
Two-Leg Raises	2 to 3 sets of 10 to 20 repetitions
Two-Arm Raises	2 to 3 sets of 10 to 20 repetitions

Shoulder

Dumbbell Presses Against the Wall	3 to 4 sets of 10 to 15 repetitions
Bent-Over Lateral Raises	3 to 4 sets of 10 to 15 repetitions
Cable Lateral Raises	2 to 4 sets of 10 to 15 repetitions

Triceps

Dumbbell Kickbacks	3 to 4 sets of 10 to 15 repetitions
Dips with Chair Seats	2 to 4 sets of 10 to 15 repetitions
Triceps Cable Push-Downs	3 to 4 sets of 10 to 15 repetitions
Seated Cable Extensions	3 to 4 sets of 10 to 15 repetitions

Chest

Dumbbell Bench Presses	3 to 4 sets of 10 to 15 repetitions
Incline Chest Presses	3 to 5 sets of 10 to 15 repetitions
Dips Between Benches	3 to 4 sets of 10 to 15 repetitions

Leg

Karate Front Stances	2 to 4 sets of 10 to 15 repetitions
Leg Extensions	2 to 4 sets of 10 to 15 repetitions
Chair Squats	2 to 4 sets of 10 to 15 repetitions
Side Squats	2 to 4 sets of 10 to 15 repetitions
Leg Curls	2 to 4 sets of 10 to 15 repetitions

Cable Workout

Do these 2 or 3 times per week.

Cable Squats	2 to 4 sets of 10 to 25 repetitions
One-Leg Cable Squats	2 to 3 sets of 10 to 25 repetitions
One-Arm Overhead Cable Extensions	2 to 4 sets of 10 to 25 repetitions

Kneeling Cable Lateral Pull-Downs	2 to 4 sets of 10 to 25 repetitions
Single-Leg Cables	2 to 4 sets of 10 to 25 repetitions

Abdominal Workout

Do these 4 to 7 days per week.

Day 1

Crunches—Hands on Knees	2 to 4 sets of 10 to 25 repetitions
Crunches—Butterfly Position	2 to 4 sets of 10 to 25 repetitions

Day 2

Seated Knee-Ups	2 to 4 sets of 10 to 25 repetitions
Hip Raises	2 to 4 sets of 10 to 25 repetitions
Toe-Touch Crunches with a Twist	2 to 4 sets of 10 to 25 repetitions

Day 3

V Sit-Ups Against the Wall	2 to 4 sets of 10 to 25 repetitions
V Sit-Ups with a Medicine Ball	2 to 4 sets of 10 to 25 repetitions

Day 4

Oblique Side Crunches	2 to 4 sets of 10 to 25 repetitions
Knees-to-Elbows Side Leg Lifts	2 to 4 sets of 10 to 25 repetitions

Day 5

Bicycles	2 to 4 sets of 10 to 25 repetitions
Medicine Ball Crunches in Front	2 to 4 sets of 10 to 25 repetitions

Day 6

Leg Raises on Elbow	2 to 4 sets of 10 to 25 repetitions
Oblique Side Crunches	2 to 4 sets of 10 to 25 repetitions

Day 7

Froggies	2 to 4 sets of 10 to 25 repetitions
Reverse Crunches	2 to 4 sets of 10 to 25 repetitions

Swiss Ball Workout

Do these 2 to 4 days per week.

Swiss Ball Crunches	2 to 4 sets of 10 to 25 repetitions
Ball Pull-Ins	2 to 4 sets of 10 to 25 repetitions

Swiss Ball Leg Raises	2 to 4 sets of 10 to 25 repetitions
Handstands	2 to 4 sets of 10 to 25 repetitions
Arm Rollouts	2 to 4 sets of 10 to 25 repetitions
Hand Walking	2 to 4 sets of 10 to 25 repetitions

Balance Drills

Do these 3 to 4 days per week.

Standing Asleep	2 to 3 sets of 30 seconds to 1 minute
Front Kicks	2 to 3 sets of 6 to 12 repetitions
Exercise Back Kicks	2 to 3 sets of 6 to 12 repetitions
Exercise Pike Position	2 to 3 sets of 30 seconds to 1 minute

Aerobics

Increase the amount of time or speed, walking 5 to 7 days per week. Add biking or cross-training to your routine 2 or 3 times per week, substituting for a walking day.

Weekly Plan

	Mon	Tues	Wed	Thur	Fri	Sat	Sun
Stretching	X	X	X	X	X		X
BackSmart Pilates	X	X		X	X		
Weights	X	X		X	X		
Cable	X		X		X		
Abs	X	X	X	X	X	X	
Aerobics	X	X	X	X	X	X	X
Ball	X	X		X	X		
Balance Drills	X	X		X	X		

YOUR BODY TYPE

It is important to stick with the fundamentals until you see how your particular body type responds to training. Different body types respond differently to training, and what works for one type will not necessarily work for another. One method of categorizing body types recognizes three fundamentally different physical types, called *somatotypes*.

- **Ectomorph.** Characteristics include a short upper body; long arms and legs; long, narrow feet and hands; very little fat storage; narrow chest and shoulders; and generally long, thin muscles.

- **Mesomorph.** Characteristics include a large chest, long torso, solid muscle structure, and great strength.

- **Endomorph.** Characteristics include soft musculature, round face, short neck, wide hips, and heavy fat storage.

Of course, no one is totally one type; most people are a combination of all three. This system of classification recognizes many subcategories, which are determined by the level of dominance of each basic category, rated on a scale of one to seven. For example, someone whose body characteristics are scored as ectomorphic—two, mesomorphic—six, and endomorphic—five would be an endo-mesomorph, basically a well-muscled jock type but inclined to carry a lot of body fat.

Proper training and nutrition can develop any body type. People with different body types may find it necessary to initially approach the training with different objectives, even though they may share the same long-term goals. This section presents some common profiles based on age, gender, and certain special conditions (people with arthritic pain, postpartum women, and those trying to lose weight) as examples of how you can use the BackSmart fitness program to suit your own needs.

Female, 23 to 35 Years

You like to work out to burn calories and trim fat or to maintain your current weight. You may also use exercise tapes at home, and you've tried many types of workout programs. You want to tone your arms, legs, and hips and strengthen your stomach region.

You usually overemphasize a specific area of the body for most of your workouts and neglect the rest of your body, which is a big mistake. By concentrating on your abs or thighs and hips, you are forcing your body to adapt to a disproportional frame, causing greater frustration and sabotaging yourself in the process. You may find yourself quitting your workouts because the exercises don't work. You obtain most of your information from fitness magazines targeted to women, and you try to apply the exact workouts, without success.

The routine suggested here can change that scenario for you by giving you a full, balanced workout while toning and shaping your hips, thighs, and midsection.

Your Program

Start your morning with the BackSmart Daily Dozen stretches and then the BackSmart Pilates. You can also do these at lunchtime, in less than 15 minutes or for as long as you like. Incorporate the balance drills throughout the day, emphasizing your breathing and concentration.

For 4 to 6 weeks, commit yourself to the following routine, and you will see improvements in your problem areas. Do the ball exercises before hitting the weights or cables, which will give you that continuous tension you need, and then do the direct abdominal exercises; try to end your workout with some moderate aerobics. You'll find that, with this routine, you will burn more calories and fat while enhancing your muscular endurance.

Sample Workout

Your workout may look something like this.

The BackSmart Daily Dozen, followed by a BackSmart Pilates workout.

Hundreds	2 to 4 sets of 25 to 50 repetitions
Corkscrews	2 to 4 sets of 10 to 25 repetitions
Scissors	2 to 4 sets of 10 to 25 repetitions
Hip Circles	2 sets of 10 to 25 repetitions
Side Leg Lifts	2 to 4 sets of 10 to 25 repetitions
Double Leg Stretches	2 to 4 sets of 10 to 25 repetitions
Jackknives	2 to 4 sets of 10 to 25 repetitions

Swiss Ball Workout

Swiss Ball Crunches	2 to 4 sets of 10 to 25 repetitions
Reverse Bridges	2 to 4 sets of 10 to 25 repetitions
Ball Pull-Ins	2 to 4 sets of 10 to 25 repetitions

Weights

Biceps

Wall/Arm Curls	2 to 4 sets of 10 to 20 repetitions
Cable Curls	2 to 4 sets of 10 to 20 repetitions

Back

Lat Pull-Downs	2 to 5 sets of 10 to 20 repetitions
Dumbbell Rows	2 to 3 sets of 10 to 15 repetitions

Lower Back

Hyperextensions on the Floor	2 to 3 sets of 10 to 20 repetitions
One-Leg/One-Arm Raises	2 to 3 sets of 10 to 20 repetitions
Two-Leg Raises	2 to 3 sets of 10 to 20 repetitions
Two-Arm Raises	2 to 3 sets of 10 to 20 repetitions

Shoulder

Dumbbell Presses Against the Wall	3 to 4 sets of 10 to 15 repetitions
Cable Lateral Raises	2 to 4 sets of 10 to 15 repetitions

Triceps

Dumbbell Kickbacks	3 to 4 sets of 10 to 15 repetitions
Triceps Cable Push-Downs	3 to 4 sets of 10 to 15 repetitions

Chest

Dumbbell Bench Presses	3 to 4 sets of 10 to 15 repetitions
Dips Between Benches	3 to 4 sets of 10 to 15 repetitions

Leg

Karate Front Stances	2 to 4 sets of 10 to 15 repetitions
Leg Extensions	2 to 4 sets of 10 to 15 repetitions
Chair Squats	2 to 4 sets of 10 to 15 repetitions
Side Squats	2 to 4 sets of 10 to 15 repetitions

Abdominal Workout

Day 1

Crunches—Hands on Knees	2 to 4 sets of 10 to 25 repetitions
V Sit-Ups Against the Wall	2 to 4 sets of 10 to 25 repetitions

Day 2

Bicycles	2 to 4 sets of 10 to 25 repetitions
Toe-Touch Crunches with a Twist	2 to 4 sets of 10 to 25 repetitions

Day 3

Seated Knee-Ups	2 to 4 sets of 10 to 25 repetitions
Hip Raises	2 to 4 sets of 10 to 25 repetitions
Toe-Touch Crunches with a Medicine Ball Twist	2 to 4 sets of 10 to 25 repetitions

Day 4

Froggies	2 to 4 sets of 10 to 25 repetitions
Leg Raises on Your Elbows	2 to 4 sets of 10 to 25 repetitions

Male, 23 to 35 Years

You worked out with weights in high school and college. Now you spend long days at the job and have less time to play or exercise on a regular basis. You may play basketball one or two times per week or on the weekend—or maybe just once or twice a month. Your goal is to build more strength, enhance your endurance, reduce the weight gain around your midsection, and strengthen your arms and chest muscles.

A top priority for men in this age-group is to concentrate on flexibility, strength, and endurance. You tend to lose your flexibility and gain weight from eating when you're not exercising.

Your Program

You should start with the BackSmart Daily Dozen and then do the prescribed shower stretches. Also include the wall stretches during your workouts: instead of sitting and resting between sets, get up and do wall stretches, which will enhance your flexibility while simultaneously improving your workout production.

Stick with the abdominal routine first in your workouts, and finish with the BackSmart Pilates as a cooldown to improve your core and add functionality to your sessions. If you dedicate two sessions a week to the cables and ball exercises and try one or two advanced stretches per week, you will see results quickly.

For your weight training, follow the intermediate or advanced program, using the priority principle to work your weakest body part first.

Male, 36 to 46 Years

You may feel that you have less endurance than you used to. You're weak in certain body parts, such as your shoulders and abdominals, and your joints hurt from time to time depending on how hard you push yourself. You want to lose the spare tire around your midsection and lower back while toning and strengthening your body without causing injury to yourself.

In this age bracket, you still can push yourself lifting heavy weights or play a sport for a few hours at a time, but you pay the price in soreness and stiffness immediately following your workout or the next day at the latest.

Your Program

You need to focus on stretching your muscles more often and during your workouts to push the lactic acid out of your muscles while training them to be more supple and adaptable to your movements.

Concentrate on the ball exercises at least three times per week to give you more dexterity and stability while firming your midsection and building strength throughout your body. Remember to work your abdominals daily, followed by stretching. Doing the cable exercises periodically as an alternative to one of your weight-training workouts will help you recover more quickly from your workouts.

Using the shower stretches daily and the BackSmart Daily Dozen stretches before going to sleep at night will help maintain your suppleness. Using the balance drills at the end of your workouts will enhance your coordination and help prevent injuries. You can also use the intermediate or advanced weight-training routines, depending on your fitness level.

Female, 36 to 46 Years

You may feel fatigue more now than in the past, regardless of your exercise or sleep routine. You may feel sorer after workouts, and certain exercises stress your joints. You gain weight easily when you don't work out consistently, and you lose your muscle definition quickly. You want to tone and shape while building strength and endurance as well as flatten your midsection.

Your Program

You need to focus on functional exercises that you can squeeze in throughout your week. Use the cable and ball workouts, followed by an abdominal routine, and conclude with balance drills.

By working with the cables and ball, you will incorporate more muscle groups in less time, while burning more calories. You will also be reducing the amount of soreness that most people in this group feel when doing only weight-training or aerobics workouts.

Do the BackSmart Pilates or abdominal workouts in the middle of your routine when you are warmed up and less likely to injury yourself. Do the wall stretches and advanced stretches at the end of your workouts, followed by the shower stretches, which will speed recovery and improve your suppleness.

Male and Female, 47 to 59 Years

Your energy level is frequently lower than it used to be, and stiffness and soreness occur more easily after you engage in sports and exercise. You want to maintain your athletic ability and tone, while losing weight.

You need to focus on building endurance and fine-tuning your fitness program to defy Father Time. You still can make serious changes to your body by building muscle and can protect your health while you lose body fat by working with your body instead of against it. With the right exercise selection and intensity, you can achieve your best condition.

As you age, hormone levels decrease, tendons weaken, collagen softens, and joint surfaces wear, causing arthritis, bursitis, and tendonitis. Probably the worst torment for individuals in this group is the loss of muscle tissue. After age 40, the average person loses about 1 percent of his or her muscle per year, which can make a huge difference in both outward appearance and strength. It can also make a difference in metabolic rate. The good news is that a consistent program of exercise and nutrition can combat, alleviate, and even reverse some of the effects of aging.

Time and again, resistance training has proved to be the best antiaging medicine around. It can prevent loss of muscle tissue, boost metabolic rate, strengthen bones, and improve balance while it promotes leanness, lowers blood pressure, and reduces other health risks. As you mature, you have to approach physical activity with more patience and employ some common sense, because your body is less forgiving now than it was when you were in your twenties. An effective fitness program after 40 doesn't have to involve the lowering of expectations, just an alteration of intention. Adapt your goals to target long-term health benefits.

Your Program

That once annoying 10- to 15-minute warm-up that you could so easily skip in earlier years now becomes all-important for your tendons and ligaments. Try to break a sweat by using the BackSmart Daily Dozen and BackSmart Pilates or abdominal movements before you start heavy training, to get the blood moving, so your body is more elastic and pliable. This will help you avoid injury and wear and tear on your joints.

Working only half of your body creates muscular imbalances that may cause back and neck pain. Men are more likely than women to lack balance in their routines and tend to work only their mirror muscles. The correct approach is to train everything equally and often. Move through each repetition slowly and deliberately, and be smart: don't injure yourself by trying to lift too heavy a weight.

Avoid anything ballistic or polymeric movements, such as jumping movements or doing Olympic-style lifts with fast, jerking motions that can harm your joints and tear muscle fibers. A steady approach to lifting will help reduce the incidence of injuries and lessen joint damage over the long term. Listen to your body, be aware of levels of fatigue and soreness, and, again, play it smart: take an extra day off between training the same body parts, and alternate free weights and cable workouts in each training session.

Incorporate the ball and BackSmart Pilates workouts throughout your routine. Do the cable exercises when you are too sore for free weights or machines. Start and end your day with the balance drills and the BackSmart Daily Dozen. These exercises will speed your recovery from your earlier workouts while enhancing your flexibility.

If you are sore after your workouts, incorporate the shower and wall stretches before you go to sleep, which further promote recovery. Use the basic or intermediate weight-training routine as your guide.

Male and Female, 60 Years and Older

People in this group want to maintain or improve endurance while preventing osteoarthritis and heart disease. Look at your workouts as a health essential, giving you more time for other activities such as golf or hiking. Emphasize flexibility and balance early in your routine, and use the ball and cable movements throughout your weekly workouts.

I cannot overstate the importance of flexibility in this particular group. Because more and more people have learned that exercising is healthy, they have flocked to the health clubs and begun exercising as if they have been doing it all their lives. As a result, this age group is probably statistically the highest for exercise-related injuries that I have seen over the past decade.

Your Program

After you are cleared to exercise by your doctor, start off slowly and focus on the BackSmart Daily Dozen and the wall stretches early on in your workouts. This will put you on the right foot to progress through your newfound fitness program and will keep you off the sidelines while your peers are exercising. If you participate in group exercise classes, be sure to do your warm-ups beforehand. I have seen many people with injuries from these types of programs because they race to the centers and jump right into the classes without taking the additional 15 to 20 minutes to stretch out their muscles.

Arthritis Pain Sufferer

Members of this group understand when I say that the summers are made for mobility and the winters are for hibernation for most arthritic pain sufferers. The cold and windy days bring the onset of stiffness and muscle soreness before you even start your morning.

It doesn't have to be that way. By following the BackSmart fitness program, you can easily start all of your days the same regardless of the season and can be functional and active year-round.

Your Program

Emphasize stretching prior to getting out of bed in the mornings, which will help you shake off any stiffness that set in during the night. Perform the

BackSmart Daily Dozen and the shower stretches before you start your morning routine. During your early afternoons, do the wall stretches to keep limber throughout your day.

Try to incorporate more cable workouts than heavy weights into your routine, which will help elongate your muscles in a functional manner, rather than just contracting against resistance. Remember to perform the balance exercises throughout your day to help protect your joints, thus preventing falls or injuries. Refer to Chapter 6 for guidelines on balance drills and other pointers.

Postpartum Woman

Giving birth causes major changes to your body, regardless of what you may have done before your pregnancy. You will have gained weight—it's only natural—and your joints may hurt more often as the result of the extra weight and the baby's position in the womb.

You need to apply the BackSmart principles to help restrengthen those muscles that carried the additional weight all those months. The program will relieve the back and leg pain stemming from your already weakened and imbalanced muscles and the stress to the joints strained by your pregnancy. The exercises will strengthen not only your abdominal muscles but also your pelvic and hip muscles, which were stressed during childbirth. Using this program, you will be rebuilding your body while burning unwanted weight in the process.

Start off slowly and build up to a full workout. Do not rush yourself back into shape; your spine as well as the muscles of your entire body have gone through a major transformation for the past nine months. With steady, consistent daily workouts, you will begin to see changes in your body shape, and your endurance will improve along with it.

Your Program

If this was your first pregnancy and you are in good health, you could start out with the basic routine without direct abdominal exercises. Always check with your doctor before beginning any exercise program. Especially if you had a C-section or had any major complications with your delivery, you may need to avoid certain exercises until you have healed completely.

Emphasizing the BackSmart Daily Dozen and wall stretches will help you get back into shape and improve the circulation in your lower body. The BackSmart Pilates in the basic routine is highly recommended; doing these movements will strengthen your body quickly without adding undue stress.

Prospective Weight-Loser—10 to 15 Pounds

A key determinant in choosing a workout for losing a targeted amount of weight is whether or not you have been exercising—and to what extent.

If you are a beginner and never used weights before, you are in for a surprise. You will melt away fat and improve tone faster than people who have been training at the intermediate and advanced levels. That's because your body will be forced to adapt to the resistance of the weights. In the weeks to come, you will notice more strength and muscle groups in your arms and legs.

Perform the exercise series from the basic routine, doing 2 to 3 sets of weight-training exercises for the first 2 weeks, followed by 3 to 4 sets the next 2 weeks, before adding weight to your exercises. The idea is to add more exercises and increase the duration of the exercise during the week to burn more calories. By the fourth week, you will notice how much easier the movements are, and you may also notice that you have dropped some pounds and exhibit subtle changes in your body. This approach will also increase your endurance and metabolism, which will help burn fat.

Your Program

Start each workout session with the BackSmart Daily Dozen stretches and BackSmart Pilates, followed by your abdominal routine. Next, use the weight-training routine specific to your level. End each session with the ball routine or cable movements to further burn calories and melt fat. Before retiring for the night, add another aerobic session to your day, such as a light walk after dinner, or another session of abdominal exercises or BackSmart Pilates followed by the wall stretches.

Remember, it is the amount of calories that you burn that counts. If you are constantly challenging your body throughout the day with mini workouts, you will burn more calories than you would by doing one long workout once a day. Abdominals and the BackSmart Pilates can be done anywhere on a moment's notice with minimal warm-up, because of the nature of the movements. Adding these workouts to your day, whenever you can, will help you lose the weight more quickly.

TRAINING LOG TO TRACK YOUR PROGRESS

The use of a training log is important in achieving your goals. The majority of people using the BackSmart program say they get valuable feedback by keeping regular track of their workouts and their overall performance. Simply writing down your workouts and daily activities in the log keeps you true to your cause and helps motivate you by showing the results you are accomplishing and/or how to head off a disaster waiting to happen.

Unlike most other training logs out there today, the BackSmart training log allows you to evaluate your progress toward your goals on a daily basis as well as for the overall week. Completing your log at the end of the day and evaluating your weekly assignment yields better results more quickly than simply trusting your memory. In fact, the whole diet industry is built on this concept of recording your daily routine to see where you may have a weakness and where your strengths lie.

Training Log Goal Sheet

Start with the accompanying goal sheet. Make copies of the form and place your completed goal sheets where you will see them every day; as you achieve your goals, you can check them off one by one, working toward your ultimate goals and eventual success.

Goal Sheet

Today's Date: ______________________

Long-Term Goal: ____

I want to achieve this long-term goal by: ______________________________

____

____

____

Short-Term Goal: ____

I will succeed in achieving this short-term goal by: ___________________

____

Short-Term Goal: ____
I will succeed in achieving this short-term goal by: __________________
____

Short-Term Goal: ____
I will succeed in achieving this short-term goal by: __________________
____

I will reevaluate my long-term goal at the 8-week mark into my new program and rate myself on a scale of 1 to 10, 10 being the best I feel at the highest improvement level.

At this point, I am:
___ making the right progress and happy with my results.
___ making some improvements in certain areas of my body; I can see changes in other areas, but only a little thus far.
___ making slow progress; I am not consistent with my workouts, and I may be eating poorly.

Reevaluate yourself in 6 to 10 weeks, and note the areas in which you are making improvement and the ones in which you are not. With your second short-term evaluation goal, you will increase your workout intensity and/or make priority changes in which body part you are working out to get that athletic body you want.

SETTING REALISTIC GOALS

Cory, 45 years old, mother of two, and die-hard tennis player for more than 25 years, did weight training to maintain her upper-body strength and worked her abdominals on the same days. She did no other aerobic activity. She came to see me because she had sustained a lower-leg injury and needed to get right back into her routine because she was scheduled to play in a tournament in a few days.

After examining Cory and ordering an MRI to rule out a rupture to her tendon, I sat down with her and helped her map out her long- and short-term goals. She was a bit surprised when I asked her what physical changes she would like to see in herself. She said she'd never thought about it and she felt as if she was in much better shape than friends her age or even younger. I asked her if any of them had sustained the number of injuries she had over the years. Her reply was, "I am much more active than they are, and of course, they don't exercise as hard as I do; I am very competitive."

That's when I pointed out that she was too hard on herself, having only one focus—tennis—and forcing everything else to revolve around her playing time. Her conditioning routine was designed by her personal trainer and was changed monthly, so as not to get stale, as she put it. After I explained to her that the trainer was giving her what she wanted, not what she needed, to keep her happy, she sat back and thought about what I had just said. I told her that if she didn't balance out her routine and start making other changes, she was looking at a shortened tennis season and future injuries down the road.

Together, we put some realistic goals down on paper. One was to compete in the tennis league with the women half her age come the following fall season, which was about six months away. A more immediate goal was to balance out her workouts both at home and in the gym. She started off with the basic level, even though she had been training with a trainer for more than 10 years. I had her doing the balance drills before her tennis practice and working her core and legs on the same day after practice. This provided her with more stability in her lower body while focusing on her muscles during her exercise routine.

I emphasized the wall exercises and stretches as part of her routine because of the upper-body tightness she had from playing a racket sport. The shower stretches and breathing exercises helped her relax and decompress, she said.

Sample Training Log: 1st Day/Basic Program

After tracking a week's worth of workouts in your training log, you can add up your scores and examine your progress. It's important to keep track of why or why not you could do your workout. This will help you not to sabotage your workouts with too many excuses.

Completed? Yes ___ No ___
Why or Why Not? ______________________________

Arm Workout

Biceps: sets ______ reps ______ weight used ______.
Wall/Arm Curl: sets ______ reps ______ weight used ______.
Triceps: sets ______ reps ______ weight used ______.
Dumbbell Kickback: sets ______ reps ______ weight used ______.

Back Workout

Dumbbell Pull-Overs: sets ______ reps ______ weight used ______.
Lat Pull-Downs: sets ______ reps ______ weight used ______.
Hyperextension on the Floor:
sets ______ reps ______ weight used ______.
One-Leg/One-Arm Raise: sets ______ reps ______ weight used ______.
Dumbbell Press Against the Wall:
sets ______ reps ______ weight used ______.
Lateral Raises: sets ______ reps ______ weight used ______.

Chest Workout

Dumbbell Bench Press: sets ______ reps ______ weight used ______.
Incline Chest Press: sets ______ reps ______ weight used ______.

Leg Workout

Karate Front Stance: sets ______ reps ______.
Two-Leg Lift with Ball Between Knees: sets ______ reps ______.

Ab Workout

Crunch—Hands on Knees: sets ______ reps ______.
Reverse Crunch: sets ______ reps ______.

Aerobics: Completed? Yes ___ No ___
Why? ____

Stretches: BackSmart Daily Dozen: Completed? Yes ___ No ___
Why? ____

Balance Drills: Completed? Yes ___ No ___
Why? ____

Rate your success in achieving your goal for the day.

Scale	**1**	**2**	**3**	**4**	**5**	**6**	**7**	**8**	**9**	**10**
	Fair				**Good**					**Excellent**

Continue with this training log for the rest of the week; at the end of the week, add up all of your scores and record the weekly total. The highest possible score is 70. Use the following guide to help interpret your rating. Each week, try to beat your previous total—or to maintain it if it is where you want to be.

- 65 to 70: **Excellent!** You're on your way to having that body and lifestyle you want. Maintain your enthusiasm, and refer back frequently to your scores each week to track your progress.

- 60 to 64: **Great!** You're being consistent in your efforts and making progress toward your ultimate goal. Charge on!

- 52 to 59: **Good!** You're taking the right steps and making an effort toward achieving your ideal lifestyle.

- 51 or below: **Fair.** Time to determine what obstacles are preventing you from reaching your goals. Make more of a commitment to yourself. Sometimes your output in a given day or week will result in skewing your number lower than it should be. Do not be hard on yourself; just be honest and you will achieve your goals.

By tracking your progress with the weekly training log, you will hopefully be a step closer to achieving your ultimate goal of that athletic body you always wanted. Remember to use all your newfound exercises to achieve your goal of becoming healthy and strong.

CHAPTER 10

HEALTHY DIET TIPS TO KEEP YOU ON TRACK

Just as not all exercise programs work for everyone, not all diets are appropriate for all people. This chapter is intended to broaden your outlook on health and food consumption and show you how you can achieve good results through a long-term, positive outlook.

I can remember numerous occasions in my childhood watching my parents struggle with so-called diets. They would go to meetings to learn about self-control and portion sizes, and my father would say to my mother, "Look at the person giving the lecture—she's as big as a house. Why should I believe her!" Or my mom would take out a scale and weigh their food before a meal, and my father would say, "I think prisoners get more food than this!" Then there was the time they came home with bags of food in special boxes; they were supposed to eat only that type of food and nothing else. My father would pop a wafer into his mouth for a snack and say, "Boy, was that good. Am I full or what?" This went on for years. They did lose weight, but they also gained it back when they got tired of following a series of difficult eating plans.

Kids today will look back and remember their parents eating their hamburgers without the buns, eliminating carbohydrates here or there, whereas only a few years ago, the whole family was eating pasta at every meal and almost no meat. As you look back at your own childhood and the food you ate and compare it with the foods you eat today, ask yourself, are they that much different?

You should certainly be buying fresh produce, but have the staple foods changed much? Open your eyes when you enter the grocery store, and keep a clear mind as you make your selections. Do you really need the extra-large size of anything? Probably not. Also, it's best to shop at least twice a week, not just once. This will help you control the urge to load up your cart as if you won't be back for weeks—and then overeat when you're at home because you're surrounded by stacks of temptation.

THINGS YOU CAN DO WEEKLY

- **Clean out your refrigerator and pantry.** Many times, people buy healthful foods and then put them away and forget about them. Because fresh foods do not have preservatives, it's best to eat them within a few days. Shopping at least twice a week, rather than just once, will allow you to buy smaller amounts of foods and bring more variety to your diet.

- **Eat for your heart during the week and for your stomach on the weekends.** Choose fish, chicken, or a vegetarian dish for your main evening meal, and you can lose weight while eating healthy. On the weekends, you can give in to your cravings a little and enjoy that fattening or sweet food. This strategy will help you maintain your goals without feeling deprived. Most people who are trying to lose weight eventually fail because they stick to a strict diet format without indulging in foods that make them happy. If you want to lose weight, be realistic; if on Wednesday you eat some cake, then when the weekend comes, eat healthy again. Remain flexible with your eating habits, and you will succeed.

- **Try eating a new food each week, either from the grocery store or at a restaurant.** By experimenting, you will develop a taste for a variety of foods, which will result in a more nutritious diet.

- **Choose more healthful foods.** Choose nonprocessed, nutritious foods (such as steamed vegetables, spinach, or broccoli) for at least two meals a day. If you eat french fries, have an apple at the same meal. Do this over several weeks, and you should be able to switch over to eating more wholesome foods rather than calorie-heavy, nutritionally empty foods.

HEALTHY DIETING

Don't be frightened by my mention of the word *diet*. This discussion is not about a drastic change or a limited regimen of special foods like the type my folks followed when I was a child; it's about the importance of adopting a lifelong, healthy way of eating. There is no need to feel deprived or hungry all the time. You may be surprised at how good you will begin feeling and looking with only a few alterations to your present eating habits.

Keeping a Food Diary

If you want to improve your eating habits, you need to start with a firm base of knowledge of how you eat now. No matter who you are, or how good you believe your eating habits are, you probably have periods when you take a turn in the wrong direction. By becoming more fully aware of your eating habits, you'll be able to catch these diversions before you grow more comfortable with the wrong choices.

Get yourself a notebook or a yellow legal pad and a pen, and without changing your normal eating habits, write down everything that passes your lips; that means even between meals. Everything counts, so write down the time, the amount, the type of food, and the course—meal or snack. For example:

9/25 10:25 A.M. Breakfast: 1 bagel with cream cheese, coffee with milk and sugar.

For the next week, do not change the way you usually eat, but continue to keep your list. This means you'll have to carry around your notebook or at least a few pages from it, so that if and when you decide to eat, you can record it. Don't wait to record it later. Don't record the food before you eat it either; often your eyes are bigger than your stomach.

If you think this is too much trouble, then maybe you should reassess whether you really want to be aware of your eating habits, how they affect the way you feel and look, and the possibility of making improvements. Decide if it is worth the trouble to look terrific and to feel terrific. It's probably not as inconvenient as you may think. If you can learn to exercise regularly and rigorously, you can also learn to eat well and healthy.

Your First Week

During the first week, write down the foods you eat each day and read back what you ate the previous day. Do you notice any patterns, either in the times you eat or in the basic types of food? Do you eat meals? As you review your food record, ask yourself if the patterns that you are beginning to see are working either for you or against you. Reading over your food diary also helps you discern any imbalances in your diet. Most of us rely too heavily on one food group—or on one food, for that matter. For the majority of us, the culprit is refined carbohydrates. These foods are easily obtainable and require little preparation. We overload on candy, sweets, cookies, and chips. An hour or so after eating the quick-energy-release foods, we feel a drop in our energy, but we tend not to associate the low with these foods, since we consumed them an hour ago. This low, or drop in energy, is caused by a sharp increase of sugar in the blood and a decrease of sugar in the muscles. It can be responsible for personality changes, fluctuating moods, and fatigue.

Near the third and fourth day of the week, you'll probably wish you could change some of your eating habits and the patterns you are seeing in your diet. They may be major problems or just minor quirks; whatever the case, these patterns can occur so often and add up so quickly that they impede your progress and keep you from reaching your goals. On your fifth through seventh days, ask yourself how you could effectively change your diet so that you will be able to make a noticeable difference and at the same time not feel as though you have given up everything. Write down the answers you come up with in your food diary.

Now, after a week or so of documenting and analyzing your food intake, you should be able to notice some specific trends in the way you eat and what days you fall off course before getting back on track. This is the time to begin putting to use what you have learned about your diet. You should have made some decisions as to what improvements need to be made.

Your Second Week

On the eighth day, eliminate one food and change or eliminate one habit in your diet that you feel will give you the best results if altered or removed. For example, let's say you eat a bowl of ice cream or a bag of chips every night while watching TV. Eliminate it. Better yet, eliminate the ice cream or chips totally from your diet for now. Don't substitute any other food at this time—unless, of course, you have been eating that particular food as a meal, in which case you might substitute a more nutritious food such as cottage cheese or fruit. If you have a habit of raiding the refrigerator in the middle of the night, or snacking so that you're not able to eat at regular mealtimes, then eliminate this habit and discipline yourself to eat at the proper times.

MAKING GRADUAL CHANGES TO YOUR DIET

These changes, as you can see, are not drastic. Nevertheless, you may find yourself feeling hungry before a meal or craving your favorite junk food at the times you ate it previously. This is because your body has adapted itself to a pattern and come to expect certain things at certain times. You can reeducate your mind and your body to adopt more healthful patterns in the same way that you educated yourself to crave ice cream or midnight snacks. The fact that a craving or feeling comes upon you doesn't mean it is healthy or necessary.

Limit Sugar Intake

For most people, cutting out sugar and foods that contain refined sugar would be the wisest first alteration to make. Read all the labels on the foods you choose: you will likely be surprised by how much sugar you consume in one day. Of course, don't cut out all sugar products on the first day; this may be too drastic a change. Instead, do it in a gradual manner, eliminating either one food or one type of food at a time. Do this every three or four days or biweekly, whichever pattern is most comfortable. These gradual changes can add up to a few pounds of weight loss; moreover, you will probably notice less bloating in your stomach area, and you will feel overall healthier and stronger in your new workout program.

Cut Down on Caffeine

Caffeine, an ingredient in soft drinks, chocolate, coffee, and many teas, would be a wise choice to eliminate or cut down on next if at all possible. Caffeine can wreak havoc with your blood sugar, often with the same effect that sugar has on your personality, energy, and appearance. Also, the acid in coffee is hard on the stomach, especially if a large amount is consumed, and too much coffee can cause nervousness and muscular tension.

When you have made your choices for the week regarding the changes that you will make in your diet, write them down in your diary. Reread them every day. Don't allow yourself to forget. After taking command of your desires and improving your present way of eating, you'll feel terrific! Continue to record your daily food intake, and make a positive effort to further improve your eating habits over the next two weeks.

Take Your Time When Eating

Think about eating more slowly, as well. If you constantly feel rushed at your job and in other areas of your day-to-day life, you may often forget to slow down when you eat. Gulping down your food can lead to overeating because you don't give your body time to tell you that you are full. It can also cause indigestion, which you'll feel throughout the rest of the day, creating more of an upset stomach. If you don't have time to eat a substantial meal, it is better to eat something light and leave some time to rest and allow the food to begin to digest. Or you can eat a smaller meal and give yourself time to eat more slowly. You won't have that stuffed feeling, but you will be satisfied.

Note the gradual alterations in your diet. Keep records and reread them daily. You should still be keeping written track of your food every time you eat. Even gum has enough sugar in it to make a difference, especially if you chew more than one piece a day.

Know the Nutritional Value in Your Food

You should have a good, comprehensive nutrition almanac that lists all the calories, carbohydrates, proteins, fats (saturated and unsaturated), and fiber content of the foods that you're eating. This almanac, accompanied by the food diary that you have been keeping, will educate you about the foods that give you better nutrition. By looking up the nutritional value of anything you're not sure of, you will gain a wealth of knowledge about the foods that you should choose when shopping and eating away from home. As you learn more about what you are eating and the healthy choices available, you will soon find that only rarely will you need to use the book for reference.

Continue to gradually eliminate foods that are not contributing to your goal. Be selective; use the nutrition almanac to determine the food value that your meals hold and what they are lacking in nutritional density. You may want to make substitutions. Also try to keep the amounts in each food group about equal.

Other Foods to Limit in Your Diet

If you are trying to get rid of excess fat, cut down on foods high in fat, salt, and carbohydrates. Begin with the grain food group, including bread. These foods are generally high in calories, salt, and carbohydrates, and when you eat more than your body can immediately use for energy, the remainder is deposited as fat. Don't be misled by some product labels, especially those that boast low fat or low carbs; no matter how much you think you know about the foods you are eating, look them up.

It might be a good idea to also record the food groups from which you are choosing, by putting a *P* in your diary by the foods that are a major source of protein, *C* by the carbohydrates, *F* by fats, and *S* for sugar content. In this way, you can see at a glance what kind of eating patterns you have adopted and can alter them if necessary.

As you reach the end of the month, you should still be keeping track of what you eat as well as eliminating the foods that will not help you reach your goal. By this time, you should have eliminated all refined sugars, refined flours, and sugar in general—unless the sugar source is fresh fruits and dairy products. Instead of refined grains, you should eat whole grains in moderation if you have lost your desired weight. And now is the time to look at your use of refined oils, such as margarine and vegetable oils. These should be eliminated and replaced with olive oil. Use small amounts of butter instead—or clarified butter for cooking. You can find the simple procedure for making clarified butter in most basic cookbooks.

You'll notice that your food is tastier when it isn't hidden under a lot of processes. Your shopping will be easier too. You will be spending less time in the grocery store, since you won't be going up and down the endless aisles of overly processed, canned, frozen, and boxed foods and can head straight for the fresh food sections.

Many processed, canned, frozen, and boxed foods have lost a lot of nutrients by the time they get to you. Fresh foods take less time to prepare, and if you buy foods that are in season, you'll also be saving money.

Healthful Snacks for Every Situation

- **For weight loss.** Include fiber and protein. Try turkey rolled in spinach or romaine leaves, or an apple with one piece of low-fat cheese.
- **To boost your energy.** Include a balance of carbohydrates and protein. Try whole-wheat bread and peanut butter, dried or fresh fruits and vegetables, oatmeal, or a handful of nuts.
- **To help lower cholesterol.** Include fiber and heart-healthy fats. Try one cup of low-fat yogurt with walnuts and orange slices, an apple, whole-wheat toast, or edamame.
- **When traveling.** Include produce and low-fat carbohydrate-protein combos. Try bags of cut-up fruits and vegetables.
- **To help you through a workout.** Include low-fiber carbohydrates and a bit of protein. Try one ounce of low-fat cottage cheese and an apple.

SAMPLE FOOD DIARY

Here's an example of what you should be writing down as you eat throughout the day, incorporating all the gradual healthy changes to your diet.

Day 1: 1/1/2005

Meal 1: 6:30 A.M.
2 boiled eggs and one-half cup of applesauce
1 cup of 2 percent milk
Multivitamin, 250 milligrams of calcium, and 250 milligrams of vitamin C
P: Eggs
C: Applesauce, milk
F: Eggs, milk
S: Applesauce, milk

Snack: 11:15 A.M.
2 slices of deli turkey
P: Turkey

Meal 2: Noon
Salad with carrots, onions, mixed greens, cucumbers, and tomatoes; low-fat dressing—blue cheese
1 cup of grilled chicken
1 glass of water
P: Chicken
C: Carrots, mixed greens, dressing
F: Chicken, dressing
S: Dressing, carrots

Meal 3: 6:30 P.M.
Grilled salmon with olive oil and butter
Boiled broccoli and one-half cup of couscous
1 glass of water
P: Salmon
C: Broccoli, couscous
F: Salmon, olive oil, butter
S: Couscous

Snack: 9:00 P.M.
One-half cup of cottage cheese
1 cup of 2 percent milk
P: Cottage cheese, milk
C: Milk
F: Cottage cheese, milk
S: Milk

Total number of protein foods for the day: 6
Total number of carbohydrate foods for the day: 8
Total number of fat foods for the day: 9
Total number of sugar foods for the day: 6

Another good method of suppressing your appetite is by doing the breathing exercises in Chapter 3 before you start your meals, which will put you at ease and allow you to relax. When you are relaxed, you have a tendency to eat more slowly and enjoy your meal rather than gulping it without tasting your food. Remember to take everything in moderation when approaching your diet, just as you do with your exercise program, which will result in your being able to stick with it and achieve your goals.

CHAPTER 11

BACKSMART TALK: INJURIES AND PREVENTIONS

Most exercise books give you the exercises and tell you how to perform them, as well as giving you a routine to go along with them. What they fail to do is address an all-too-common mistake: exercising too much! For most people, overexercising results in their giving up on their workouts. I know I just devoted an entire book to explaining to you how to do movements that will build strength; enhance your flexibility, endurance, and balance; and sculpt your body while preventing future injuries—but most people go overboard!

Determining the most effective exercises for people with back and neck problems is not always easy. Exercise is an important key to full recovery of function, so I am inclined to recommend all appropriate exercises. As a result, people usually wind up with an extensive list of exercises, including stretching, strengthening, stabilizing, and coordinating movements. In reality, however, most people have a limited amount of time (and enthusiasm) to put the exercises into practice.

When preparing an exercise program that will be most effective for you, don't overwhelm yourself with trying to decide which exercises you should be doing; use the BackSmart plan as an outline for your workouts. Unfortunately, it seems that the more knowledgeable people are about exercise, the more likely they are to overcomplicate the process. Don't get bogged down in the details—counting repetitions on every set, starting with the same amount of weight as you did in your last workout. Listen to your body. If doing two sets fatigues your muscles, do not complete another two sets simply because you did the last time and you want to follow your workout plan exactly as before.

OVERCOMING OBSTACLES THAT LEAD TO INJURIES

Let's look at some major issues that can affect your ability to stay on track and to recognize and avoid the pitfalls that most people encounter when exercising. In treating and training people of all age-groups and physical abilities, I have found the conditions discussed here to be the chief obstacles. You should also frequently review the chapters on proper body positions to help prevent injuries.

The Road to Preventing Overload

The condition commonly referred to as overload occurs when people perform too many exercises, even if they train briefly once a day. Typically, the victim of overload strongly believes in the benefits to be gained from these various exercises and is eager to see results. Problems begin the next day, when it becomes clear that the amount of commitment is simply not compatible with the person's current lifestyle.

The most effective way to begin an exercise program is to start small and follow through consistently. This means that you start with one or two exercises that you really feel comfortable doing and perform them frequently. Once-a-day exercising is the quickest and easiest way to establish a regular routine. You can fit the session into your daily schedule whenever it's best for you—mornings, during lunch breaks, or evenings.

Initially, you will do exercises limited to light weights and stretching, so the traditional "day of rest in between" is not needed. You want to establish a new habit of regular, consistent exercising. You are taking small steps to success when you incorporate exercise into your daily lifestyle and set achievable goals. With this approach, success will come your way, and the direct benefits will be apparent.

Soreness

Another important area that is given little attention is soreness. Not a day goes by without my hearing about soreness from one of my patients when I recommend a new exercise or from an athlete at one of my conditioning seminars. They describe their soreness as if they never knew they had those muscles in their bodies. This is also the reason most people quit exercising, because they are not used to the new discomfort. Let's face it: the majority of people strive for pleasure in life—not pain, which we run from. But the crux of the matter is that you have to differentiate between harmful pain and soreness that results from retraining your body, by adding the right amount of stress, which means not going overboard.

By using the BackSmart method, you will have control of the level of your discomfort and ways to get around the pain you may feel in your back or neck. This will allow you to enhance your body's ability to adapt and to overcome obstacles that would otherwise prevent you from progressing with your fitness goals. The following tips will help you evaluate your soreness and recover more quickly from your workouts and stay on track.

- Are you sore from using the machines or working out with free weights, making it difficult to move your limbs without pain? If so, then use only cables or your body weight for resistance in your next workout or two, before returning to the machines or free weights.

- If your midsection is sore from your abdominal workout, try doing the BackSmart Pilates workout instead and gradually add back the abdominal exercises.

- Do more of the balance and ball movements at the beginning and end of your workouts to help prevent the lactic acid from pooling into your muscles; this will speed recovery.

- Use moist heat (hot showers, whirlpool) after your workouts for 10 to 15 minutes to help relax your muscles. *This is not recommended if you have high blood pressure or are pregnant or have any other related health risk to high heat.*

- Repeat your BackSmart Daily Dozen stretches and shower stretches at the end of your workout and again before you go to sleep.

- Don't assume that you'll improve your fitness by working out longer.

- Finally, if you are too sore and you can't move without feeling like the Tin Man, you need to go lighter in your next workout or skip a day of resistance training completely. Instead, emphasize your stretching and balance movements, which will help speed your recuperation time.

Dehydration

When it comes to overtraining, one of the sure signs of doing too much is dehydration. The problem is of particular concern to people who are trying to lose weight and think they should sweat it off. When your body is in a dehydrated state, you have lost water and important blood salts such as potassium and sodium. Vital organs such as the kidneys, brain, and heart cannot function without a minimum of water and salt.

If you experience any of the following symptoms while exercising or afterward, increase your fluid intake immediately.

- Thirst and/or a dry mouth or lips
- Rapid and/or weak pulse
- Sunken eyes or failure of skin to bounce back quickly when lightly pinched and released
- Confusion, dizziness, and lethargy
- Low urine output; concentrated urine—appears dark yellow

It's better to drink small amounts of fluids throughout the day than to consume a large amount before and after a workout.

Pain

Pain when you're training is a warning sign that an area has been injured. By letting the pain be your guide, you can practice preventive medicine. First, avoid the activity that caused the pain, allowing the area involved to recover. After an adequate period of rest, you can gradually resume the activity that caused the injury. Once you have regained full range of motion of the injured extremity or other body part and there is no associated pain, you've healed enough to increase the resistance to that movement on a gradual, progressive basis.

If you begin to feel pain again, you have gone too far. Healing takes place by degrees over time, and pain is an indicator of how far along you are. If you do not stay within the boundaries described and do too much too soon, instead of gaining freedom from pain, you will run the risks of reinjury, which can lead to a more severe and chronic injury.

Exercisers often become frustrated with prolonged or even short recuperation periods because of the loss of conditioning, the setbacks, the muscle atrophy, and the mental and emotional anguish of not being able to do their workouts at their previous intensity. However, both the ability to deal competently with injury and the discipline to allow the healing to take place are essential to your success in achieving your ultimate goals.

Resting

Rest is also important and is often one of the more overlooked and deprived parts of people's lifestyle. The majority of us would love to sleep longer if we could, but our daily routines don't allow it. So, if you can't get that magical eight hours of sleep each night, I recommend taking catnaps throughout the day. Five to 10 minutes at lunchtime or whenever possible will help refresh your body and make you feel like doing more during the day.

Having Fun

Many of the exercises presented in this book will be challenging for you at first. Don't be deterred or embarrassed. Remember when you were a kid and had no inhibitions? Try to summon that attitude. Allow yourself to have fun rolling on the ball or standing tall while raising your leg in a balance position. Visualize yourself as a ballet dancer or martial artist. Rise to the competitiveness inside you when using the BackSmart method; don't be distracted by any negative comments about your newfound lifestyle. Remember what motivated you in the first place. Enjoy yourself and have fun with the exercises. I have been teaching these movements to adults, athletes, and children for years, and to see the smiles on their faces from just knowing they have reached and accomplished a movement when only a few weeks before they could barely move is a joy for all involved.

Start practicing healthful eating and regular exercise habits today. Procrastination will get you nowhere. Be smart and safe, and make sure you get plenty of rest. Good luck and have fun.

CAUSES OF INJURIES

To become successful, you must constantly try to push beyond your physical limits. The downside is that there is always a chance you will exceed the ability of your physical structure to endure the strain. This can result in injury. Some injuries are so slight and so common that you barely take notice of them. Others are more serious and require the attention of a physician. Progress for anyone is dependent on good physical health, and an injury can lead to a serious setback. Therefore, it is important to understand the types of injuries that might occur, how to prevent them, how to work around them, and what can be done to treat them and rebuild the injured area.

The body is a highly complex physical and biochemical mechanism, one that is subject to a variety of injuries, and each individual is susceptible to specific types of injuries. Injuries usually occur at the weakest place along a given structure—in the muscle, at the muscle and tendon juncture, along a tendon, at the tendon bone attachment, in a ligament, at a joint. Sometimes injuries occur over time because of overuse, and sometimes they happen because of an acute episode, such as mishandling a heavy weight.

In dealing with the subject of injuries, it is important to be technically and medically accurate. The medical concepts and vocabulary involved may be difficult to differentiate and comprehend, but as a dedicated exerciser, you need to have access to this information to help prevent, treat, and avoid recurrence of physical injuries. Therefore, I have divided the following sections into technical and practical information. The technical information will provide you with a clinical explanation of how the muscle, tendon, joint, and ligament structures of the body can be injured and what can be done to prevent and repair the various kinds of strains and sprains that can accompany intense physical training. The practical information will give you a look at the most common injuries to specific body parts and how to deal with them.

MUSCLE AND TENDON INJURIES

Tendons connect your voluntary muscles (the ones you actually contract to do something) to the bone. *Tendinous connective tissue* is found at both ends of a muscle (tendons of origin and tendons of insertion). Injuries to the muscle or tendon can occur in several ways. One way is by direct trauma, such as a blow from a blunt or sharp object, causing a bruise or a cut. Another way that you will most likely encounter injuries while exercising is from strain caused by overworking these structures or by a single violent episode, such as a sudden stretching force applied to a muscle that is in the act of vigorous contraction when the force applied is stronger than the structure's ability to withstand tearing. The tear may be complete or partial and can occur at the *musculotendinous junction*, in the tendon, or where the tendon attaches to the bone.

Sometimes a small piece of bone is pulled off and left attached to the end of the tendon. This is known as an *avulsion fracture*. In a sense, the muscle or tendon is overpowered by the amount of resistance you are working against, and the area of least resistance is the site of your injury. The degree of injury, whether mild or severe, depends on the force of the contraction and the amount of resistance used. A few fibers may be torn, or the entire structure may be disrupted. This is the main reason I caution you not to go overboard with using too heavy a weight in your exercise program.

In most cases, the strain is mild, simply an overstretching of the muscles, with no appreciable tearing. This would result in pain and discomfort with your movement, along with a subsequent muscle spasm, guarding the injured area. In more severe injuries with actual tearing of the fibers, symptoms are increased. Pain and discomfort are more severe, there is swelling in the region, and you have limited movement.

Tendinitis

People commonly misapply the term tendinitis to their injuries. In reality, most injuries you are going to incur are strain, whereas tendinitis is an inflammatory condition of the tendon that usually results from overuse of the particular area and can sometimes be caused by a lack of circulation in the area.

One of the most common examples is *bicepital tenosynovitis*, which involves the tendon of the long head of your biceps, in the bicepital groove in the shoulder. The early symptom is shoulder pain, which may be present only with motion as the tendon passes back and forth in the sheath, or may be constant and occur even at rest.

I have found that one of the best treatments for tendinitis is to apply ice to the inflamed area for one minute and then moist heat for seven minutes, twice a day. This is another injury in which the area should not be trained until it is fully healed.

Muscle Spasm

Spasm is a term applied to involuntary contractions of the muscles (spasm and strain are not the same). Nerve pressure and lack of circulation also contribute to this problem. Muscle spasm is another sign of a strain. This sudden and often violent contraction of the muscle is a protective reflex that, in a sense, is guarding that area against further motion until there has been time for recovery. The spasms may last for an extended period, from several hours to days, and can cause a great deal of pain.

Common remedies include applying ice or moist heat to the trouble area, increasing the intake of minerals, especially calcium, and stretching the major muscles in the affected area. If you experience muscle spasms, ask yourself if you were dehydrated or if you failed to stretch out thoroughly before your workout.

Muscle Cramps

Cramps, on the other hand, are a contraction that usually comes and goes rapidly, the result of overuse and fatigue. They can also be caused by nerve pressure and/or calcium, magnesium, or potassium deficiency. You feel muscle cramps usually after resting and then when you attempt to move or use that muscle group again vigorously. Rest and protection against further injury may be all that is required.

In the early stages, you use the same treatment protocol as for a muscle strain: rest, moist heat, and protection against further injury. Also, doing the BackSmart Daily Dozen stretches throughout the day will help push the lactic acid out of your muscles and speed your recovery time.

Strain

A strain is a muscle tendon injury and is one of most common injuries among athletes, especially those who do resistance training with too heavy a weight. The most common area for a strain to occur is where the tendon meets the bone, such as the quadriceps or the biceps, which are attached at the joints. Use the same treatment protocol as for a muscle strain.

Spinal Pain

There is a direct connection between reduced spinal stability and spinal pain. Spinal stability is directly influenced by three major functional areas. The first is the spinal tendons, ligaments, and joints. The second is the muscular system surrounding the spine. The third is the control of the muscular system and the joints by the nervous system. Damage to the muscular system or failure in the way the muscles are activated by the nervous system, combined with injuries to the joints, tendons, or ligaments, causes spinal instability, leading to spinal pain. These functions are all interlinked; each one is reliant on the next and will compensate in certain ways for deficiencies in one or the other. If there is a problem in one of these systems and the other systems have failed to compensate, injuries and spinal pain will result.

JOINT AND LIGAMENT INJURIES

Movement occurs at a joint where two bones come together. The articulating parts of the joints, the parts that come in contact with each other, are composed of cartilage, a smooth, gristlelike substance. Cartilage allows for a smooth gliding motion of one part of the joint on the other. Softening or fraying of this smooth joint surface is often the first step in a long chain of events leading to early degenerative arthritis, the degeneration of the bone and cartilage of a joint, which is a painful and a chronically disabling condition. Also, athletes who incur cartilage and bone fractures in their playing days may suffer from degenerative joint disease as they age.

Ligaments are tough, fibrous bands that connect two bones. They help to stabilize the joint and prevent abnormal joint motion while allowing motion to proceed in the normal functional direction. The ligaments are the passive stabilizers of your joints, as opposed to the muscle and tendon group, which are your active stabilizers. The degree of a given injury depends on the amount of force applied and the inherent strength of the structures involved. Only a few ligament fibers may be torn, or the ligament may be partially or completely disrupted. Usually, if you experience slight pain and few symptoms, the damage is minor. If there is considerable pain and the swelling and discomfort are more noticeable, the injury is more severe.

Sprain

A sprain is a ligament injury. It can be caused by overstretching the ligaments while under stress or by too much twisting in the areas around the joints, which can lead to partial tearing of the fibers. A sprain is one of the few problems that require you to stop training the area involved. If you continue to train the injured area, you will most likely aggravate the injury and cause further damage and future complications. You should rest the area and the surrounding muscle groups to prevent further harm, and seek professional help if it does not heal quickly.

Bursitis

Bursitis is inflammation of the *bursa*, a saclike cavity in the joint containing synovial fluids to protect the joint from locking up. A bursa provides a lubricated surface where a tendon glides directly over the bone. Bursitis is a condition in which, through wear or other causes, the bursa is not able to do its job, and movement in the area causes pain and difficulty. Each joint contains multiple bursas, and isolation of the particular bursa that is inflamed has to be done by a skilled practitioner. Such joint problems can be greatly aggravated by training on machines that restrict the normal movement of the joint. This is another reason to make sure you properly fit the equipment when exercising.

Scoliosis

Scoliosis is not a disease but rather a condition relating to the shape of the spine. A normal spine has an S-curve shape when viewed from the side. A spine with scoliosis has overcompensated with curves usually in the upper or lower regions or both. In severe cases, the spine tends to rotate and place pressure on the ribs.

Abnormal curvature of the spine affects less than 5 percent of the population, but the incidence increases with older age-groups for many reasons unrelated to scoliosis. The most common type of scoliosis is idiopathic, which means "without cause." Idiopathic scoliosis occurs more frequently in girls than boys. It usually first appears between the ages of 9 and 12. People with scoliosis have asymmetric body proportions, such as one shoulder higher than the other, but for the most part, this is undetectable without an x-ray. Most of us have a slight increase or decrease curve in the spine, and having scoliosis does not put you at greater risk of developing back or neck pain. My patients have benefited tremendously from using the BackSmart plan to strengthen and tone their bodies and help prevent future injuries. The exercises help to restore proper balance and flexibility to the body, which is what is needed.

Arthritis

Let me reassure you that the BackSmart exercises won't hurt you if you have osteoarthritis or rheumatoid arthritis. In fact, they will help you prevent muscular loss and further wear and tear on your joints. Another benefit is the temporary pain relief from performing movements such as the wall stretches and shower stretches, which reduces the stress on your joints.

However, you must be careful not to use too heavy a weight or perform too many sets of any particular movement. You are the best judge of what works for you, so let any discomfort be your guide. If you feel uncomfortable doing any exercise, cut the number of repetitions in half at the beginning and slowly work your way into the workouts.

PREVENTING INJURIES

Most injuries happen because of poor mental concentration, incorrect training or overtraining, or failure to stretch and warm up properly.

Concentration and Focus

Regardless of what you're doing, mental concentration is a prerequisite for success. Whatever you do, the results are realized in direct proportion to the amount of concentration you exert. If you're trying to concentrate on two things at the same time, such as working out and talking, you're not putting all of your energy into either. To progress and move on to heavier weights and push yourself further in your workouts, you have to put all of your energy into your form, sets, and reps. As soon as your mind wanders and you pick up a heavier weight and begin training without full concentration, you're setting yourself up for an injury.

Whenever your training program becomes too routine, the challenge is lost and it's time to revise the program or move forward to a more advanced program. By avoiding the same routine in your training, you can sharpen your concentration, which is crucial to your success and healthy outcome.

Correct Training

"An ounce of prevention is worth a pound of cure" should be the rule for everyone who exercises. There's a fine line between overuse and chronic strain due to the intensity levels in your workout. Intense workouts are bound to lead to occasional residual muscular soreness or soreness of the muscle and tendon complex. This kind of overuse is not exactly an injury, and most exercisers take it as a sign that they have actually trained hard enough.

Most everyone who comes to me for professional help about a training injury has been overtraining. When this happens, the body is more susceptible to injury. You cannot make progress if you are overtraining. The most common telltale signs of overtraining are the following:

- Feeling flat and muscles not responding during a workout
- Fatigue
- Lower resistance to infections or colds
- Lack of concentration
- More than the usual amount of aches and pains from training
- Less desire for training, and lack of motivation

Incorrect training causes an imbalance in the body. This is why I recommended that you follow the training programs in the sequences given in this book. Some muscle groups have to be trained more, and some less; otherwise, the entire structure is thrown out of balance, and a weakness in certain areas of the body is created, which can easily set you up for an injury.

Proper exercise form is another factor that will help you avoid injury. If possible, look at yourself in a mirror while you are training, to be sure that your movements are smooth and flowing. Or have someone watch you exercise and check your form against the form shown in the book. If your movements are jerky or if you throw your body around in completing a movement, you're injuring yourself.

Resistance training, like lifting weights, causes the muscles to become more contracted. This type of exercise, combined with normal daily activities, contributes to muscle spasms. Therefore, the muscles need to be stretched before, during, and after training. Use the BackSmart Daily Dozen stretches or the wall stretches.

Proper Warm-Up and Stretching

If you are so sore that you can hardly move and the intensity of your substantial workouts is diminished, you've probably gone too far. Muscles that are tight, tired, and sore are more vulnerable to injury. If you insist on working out even under these conditions, there's a good chance that you will pull or tear some part of the muscle and tendon complex. The best prevention under these circumstances is gradual stretching, warm-ups, or, when the condition is severe, keeping the workouts light.

Stretching involves the entire muscle and tendon complex, lengthening it so that you reduce the chance of an exercise movement's suddenly stretching these structures past their limits and causing damage. In cooler weather, it is important to warm up longer. Using the shower stretches after your workouts is highly recommended as part of your cooldown routine after your training session. When you warm up properly, you pump blood and oxygen to the area and literally raise the temperature of the muscles involved, allowing them to contract with greater force. The best way to avoid training injuries is to take care to stretch and warm up before, during, and after working out and to observe proper technique when training with weights.

PREVENTION FOR SPECIFIC INJURED AREAS

The stronger you are, the more strain you're able to put on your muscles and tendons, but often the muscles become stronger at a faster rate than the tendons, thus creating an imbalance that can cause problems in the future. You must allow yourself to progress at a reasonable rate. Beware of training too intensely or with too much weight and without proper preparation.

Lower Back

Approximately 90 million Americans suffer from lower-back problems. When people are training with weights, lower-back problems are usually caused by improper abdominal exercises and poor posture positions. I designed the training program in this book to avoid lower-back problems; however, it is essential to use correct form while training and to refrain from any jerky or explosive movements.

It is possible to strain the spinal erectors or other lower-back muscles by overstressing the area, especially when you do a movement that hyperextends the lower back—such as bench presses or leg raises for the abdominal region, in which the lower back is lifted clear off the bench and hyperextended. A certain amount of curvature in the lower-back region is normal, but bending it too far under stress can cause facet joint and disk problems. Many patients have come in after exercising on equipment that didn't fit them adequately. Machines have a range to accommodate people of certain sizes, and if you happen to be beyond that range—either too tall or too short—you are likely to injure yourself. Using dumbbells offers less restriction, thus optimizing alignment of the spine. Using dumbbells makes exercising both safer and more effective, since you are bringing the weights to you rather than trying to make your body fit a machine. I recommend starting with free weights and a cable workout, and then gradually adding machines into your routine.

When you strain your lower back, you may feel pain radiating down into your hips and legs or upward toward your middle back. Sometimes these muscles will go into spasm to prevent further injury. You can also have a sprain in the lower back when there is an injury to the ligaments in the area. It may be difficult for you to tell whether you have incurred a sprain or a strain, but in any event, the treatment is virtually identical.

Another lower-back injury you can incur is a ruptured disk. The disks are situated in between the vertebrae, and when they rupture, the pulp material inside the disk can extrude and press on the nerves. You may feel pain anywhere along the back or even down into the legs, but it is this specific pressure that causes the pain, and treatment involves alleviating that pressure. One specific type of nerve problem is *sciatica*. The two sciatic nerves are the largest nerves of the body, extending from the spine all the way down the leg, and when pressure is put on the sciatic nerve, the pain is severe and disabling.

As mentioned earlier in the discussion of proper body mechanics while exercising, many people suffer unnecessarily by incorrectly working or overworking the abdominal region. An example is using improper leg and back positions when performing leg raises or crunches. Remember to follow the guidelines for the BackSmart Pilates and abdominal exercises in Chapter 5 to prevent stress to your lower back.

The most important rule to remember if you have suffered from a lower-back injury is to avoid all pressing exercises and back exercises involved in supporting your weight and resistance. Avoid doing abdominal movements until your lower back has recovered. Using the wall stretches and the BackSmart Daily Dozen should be your first priority. Use the breathing exercises in Chapter 3 to help relax your deep muscle groups in your core region. Consult with a doctor of chiropractic to determine when you should continue resuming your regular routine.

The most common injuries come from the muscles being strained and the ligaments being sprained. When this occurs, the vertebrae have moved out of position, and a slight displacement of the bone takes place. These phenomena also involve the extremities. The common term for this is a *pinched nerve*, which means there is pressure on the particular nerve or group of nerves, and the nerve supply from the brain and spinal cord to the organ or extremity is diminished.

In my practice, I have found pinched nerves to be especially prevalent among people who use a lot of heavy weights in their routines. Any lifting, particularly squats and overhead presses, causes compression in the lower back. In many instances, this compression results in problems with the legs such as sciatica or muscle weakness. Sometimes the legs even diminish in size if the injury goes untreated for a long time; the muscle can actually atrophy. When the normal spinal function is restored, the symptoms usually become reversible and the body returns to normal. Sometimes certain exercises have to be eliminated, however, or the problem will continue because of the constant aggravation and stress on the weakened body part.

Upper Back

Any of the upper-back muscles may be subject to strain: the trapeziuses, levatores, rotator cuff muscles, and lats all can be pulled or pushed beyond their capacity by your using too heavy a weight or doing too many exercises in a workout or simply not being thoroughly stretched out and warmed up.

It can be difficult to say which particular muscle has been overstressed. You may feel pain when you turn your head, lift your chin a certain way, or raise your shoulders and arms at a certain angle or height. Often you will contract these muscle groups and pull on them at the same time, which may lead to overstress and to some degree of muscle tear. If the injury is not too severe, it is not necessary to know precisely which muscles are affected. Simply rest the area and use the appropriate treatment.

Neck

Neck problems are common among people who do weight training or engage in sports that involve following the movement of a fast-moving ball or similar object. For instance, if you play golf, you look down at the ball to hit it and turn your head in the direction it went to follow its course. Because you usually do not swing from both sides, you develop some form of muscular imbalance. Usually the trapeziuses are too strong and the anterior neck muscles are too weak.

Neck problems can be aggravated by shoulder presses and by holding your hands behind your neck while performing crunches during abdominal movements. These exercises should be eliminated from your workout until the symptoms subside. When doing abdominal work, follow the guidelines discussed in Chapter 5 for the correct hand placement, and slowly ease back into your routine.

Shoulders

Shoulder injuries are frequent occurrences among exercisers. The two exercises that most often lead to a shoulder injury are the overhead press and the bench press. Shoulder presses put a particularly high degree of stress on the shoulders. Heavy stress can cause partial tearing of the rotator cuff muscles and the surrounding tendons. It is also possible to overstress any part of the three heads of the deltoids or their tendons of insertion or origin. Another possible problem in the shoulder area is bursitis.

The shoulder is the only joint in the body that is supported by the muscles. I have advised using the cable movements with different starting positions to emphasize all the muscles in your shoulder joint. You now have a variety of movements from which to choose using free weights, machines, or the cable to build a stronger shoulder region. Remember to include the functional movements with the ball to enhance your stability in this vulnerable region. Use lighter weights and concentrate on good form early on in your workout.

Elbows and Other Joints

The elbows are subjected to constant stress whenever you do pressing movements. In addition to the acute problems that can result from overstressing the joint by using heavy weights or sloppy technique, a certain amount of cumulative damage occurs over months and years of heavy training, sometimes resulting in degenerative arthritis. This kind of degenerative problem can occur in other joints, such as the shoulders or knees, and is difficult to detect in the early stages, since it can come on too slowly to be immediately noticeable. Gradually increasing degrees of pain can be one symptom; an increasing limitation of range of motion is another indicator. Either of these suggests some damage to the internal structure of the elbow, which, if left untreated, may eventually become irreversible.

Triceps

Triceps are subject to the same sorts of strains as the biceps and other muscles. A common triceps injury is *olecranon bursitis*. When you do extension movements like triceps extensions or use improper technique on the bench press movement, you pull on the insertion of the triceps, at the elbow. This overlies a bursa, which can become irritated when a lot of stress is put on the area and produce a burning sensation. Triceps can also be strained by overtraining or by sudden stress due to poor training technique in racket sports and golf. In cases of a complete tear of the triceps, surgery would be required to repair the structure.

Wrists

Wrist problems are usually due to an imbalance in the forearm muscles or to flexing the hand too far back toward the elbow. Hanging wrist curls will assist in balancing the muscles and correcting the causes of wrist injuries.

Chest Muscles

Strains in the chest muscles most often occur among exercisers who like to bench-press as heavy as they can. This type of strain is often associated with overstressed muscles due to handling too heavy a weight as well as with failing to warm up properly. Poor technique also accounts for a high proportion of chest injuries. Dropping the weight too quickly while doing a bench press can cause a heavy and sudden jerk to the whole chest region. Similarly, dropping the weights too quickly when executing dumbbell flies can also overstress the chest muscles, especially if the muscles are tight and have not been warmed up and stretched before the workout.

INITIAL TREATMENT

Initial treatment for all of these injuries is rest, and the injured area must be protected against further injury. Working through or working out the injury can only make it worse. For a mild strain, rest and avoid the activity that caused injury. This may be the only treatment necessary until the region has recovered. In more severe cases, crutches may be required for a leg injury, or a sling or splint may be necessary for complete or partial elimination of weight on an injured arm. Bed rest may also be required, with elevation, compression, wrapping, and use of ice packs. If the injury occurs in a non-weight-bearing extremity, the same logic applies.

In severe muscle and tendon injuries, with complete rupture of the components, the integrity of these components must be restored, and surgical repair may be required. *Do not attempt to self-diagnose a serious injury or treat it on your own.* The worst advice you can get is usually found at the gym. Immediately seek out professional help if you are unsure of the cause of your pain.

REMEDIES FOR BACK AND NECK PAIN

Most back and neck pain doesn't come from a single physical episode or injury. It is a result of stresses over time that build up during everyday activities. Inevitable minor abuse is compounded by the normal wear and tear on your body; then one day, a routine activity or a familiar prolonged posture may push your body a little too far, and the pain begins.

The neck and back pain remedies that work for some people do not necessarily work for others; there's no universal solution. One benefit of this program is that you focus on all aspects of fitness. So, by working on flexibility, strength, endurance, balance, and coordination, you will achieve a more fit and athletic body. Yes, there are a number of things you can do to control your pain. First, you can use either ice or heat, whichever works better. Again, since people respond differently to different therapies, there's no set rule. I recommend ice in the summer and heat in the fall and winter. The biggest mistake people make is leaving the ice or heat on too long. A general rule is 10 minutes on, followed by 15 minutes off. The most effective treatment is alternating hot and cold on an hourly basis, until you can do some light stretches. Doing the shower stretches, which are designed to relieve most aches and pains, is another option; it all depends on what you prefer.

What Can Help

Chair

There is no such thing as a perfect chair. People come in different shapes and sizes, and we all move and sit differently. Each individual will compensate differently from the next person suffering from similar pain. However, there are a few guidelines that you may want to follow regarding the chair of choice.

First, find one that supports the small of your back and its normal curve. There should be a balance between firmness and give to the chair, and the back of the chair should tilt forward and backward a few degrees, to suit your comfort level. Certainly, prolonged sitting in front of a computer will cause most people to stiffen up, no matter how well designed the chair may be; if you remain immobile for long periods, you are inviting discomfort and pain. No matter how good the chair is, it is smart to take breaks every half hour or so and do the BackSmart Daily Dozen stretches or the wall stretches for a few minutes.

Pillow

Some cervical pillows are designed with special foam or firmness in the lower half that is used to fill the gap between your ear level and your shoulder. This structure can give you that added support you need for a good night's rest. You can also use a rolled-up towel with the same effect. I recommend a comfortable pillow that will displace the weight of your head. Another technique you can try is to lie on your side, with a pillow between your legs just above your knees. Placing a pillow between your legs helps maintain the alignment of your spine and hips. This prevents you from twisting your hips, which causes stress to the lower-back region. Finally, keep in mind that, like your clothes, pillows need to be replaced when they show wear.

Mattress

With more than one-third of your life spent in bed, the selection of a bed is an important decision. The availability of a wide variety of mattresses, all making different claims, can make your search exhausting and confusing.

Have you ever thought about how important your bed is to your well-being—what role it plays in your health, your level of daily activity, and your overall energy level? It's a fact that how you sleep plays a large part in how you feel the next day. On any given night, more than a third of all people have trouble sleeping. For many of them, all it takes to cure the problem is the right bed. If you've ever awakened with a stiff neck or an aching back, you should know how important correct sleep posture is. A good bed can mean the difference between sleeping well and waking up tired and sore. You need a supportive environment to allow your body to heal itself naturally during resting hours.

Do you know why you've been told to sleep on a firm bed all these years? Historically, mattresses were very soft and tended to sag in the middle, forcing people to sleep in a hammock position. To no surprise, people would complain about back problems. The remedy suggested was to place a board under the sagging mattress for better support. Thus the myth of the firm mattress was born. However, extensive research in the bedding industry has given way to the truth. It is now commonly accepted that a firm mattress is inflexible and unsupportive, causing discomfort and pain in the back, neck, shoulders, and hips. A firm bed forces the body to conform to it, which means the spine must adopt an unnatural position. When you try to rest your shoulders against a hard surface, your body is tilted upright, your shoulders pinch inward toward your hips, and, as a result, your spine is bowed. In fact, if your shoulders are not allowed to sink in, it will be virtually impossible to align your lower back. In addition, sleeping on a firm mattress creates pressure points, which can contribute to poor circulation.

Go to the stores and try out a number of different types of beds. Do not be swayed by sales or endorsements from associations. After finding the bed you think is the most comfortable, return two or three days later and see if the same bed still feels right to you. I know this sounds like a lot of effort, but I think it's worth it. You will likely be living with your choice for many years to come, and you should be completely satisfied with your decision.

What to Avoid

If you have back pain, you should avoid wearing shoes with high heels. For most people, elevating the heels increases the curve in the lower back, causing more pressure to the spine. Wearing flat shoes is more supportive and helps prevent backaches, which is especially important if you'll be standing for prolonged periods.

Carrying too much weight in your arms or on your body is another contributor to back pain. Students who carry backpacks around all day are putting a lot of extra load on their bodies, and compensation usually occurs in the form of posture changes as the weight becomes burdensome. The same applies to carrying laptops, suitcases, and handbags. Make sure you need all that stuff that you are toting around in the first place, and remember to switch sides when carrying anything, to help compensate for any imbalance that may occur. Also, stretch your muscles frequently so that they do not bunch up on you due to the load, allowing you to operate effectively and without stress, strain, injury, or pain. Soon you will begin to do what you need to do without a second thought.

A cervical collar or lumbar support belt can provide short-term comfort, primarily by giving you a feeling of protection and a physical barrier to moving too far too quickly. Some back braces may help support the way you lift a certain object from one spot to another, but they do not replace good muscle tone and strength. I strongly recommend not using these devices, because they create a false sense of security, and you may overexert yourself and cause more pain in the process. Also, to overcome neck or back pain, you must keep moving, and the cervical collar and back braces tend to have the opposite effect.

Exercises to Avoid

Throughout this book, I have attempted to make you aware that no matter what happens to your body, it tries to maintain balance and equilibrium.

This tendency applies to the body's structure as well as its organs. Your body always tries to keep going and to function as normally as possible in every situation. Thus, as soon as an imbalance is created in the body, it is immediately more susceptible to various injuries. I have seen several exercises done repeatedly that actually cause imbalances in the body's structure, and I have listed the most common ones here. These exercises are of no benefit to your body and could cause more harm than good, no matter at what fitness level you are.

- Jumping jacks
- Exercises involving any form of twisting of the spine, including those performed while you are lying down
- Side bends involving holding free weights
- Wide-grip bench presses and wide-grip incline presses
- Pull-downs to the back of the neck
- Any abdominal exercises using weights
- Any exercises on a low-back machine

Also, avoid using the back machine at your gym. Once again, if you do not fit the machine exactly right, you're putting yourself at risk for serious injury. These machines isolate a region in your body that is already weak, and forcing a load onto it will cause damage. The lower back is made to work in sync with the legs and upper body, as a unit. Use the floor exercises in the home gym workout and the BackSmart Pilates instead.

Many of my patients with back and neck pain have asked me over the past few years if yoga is safe. I think that for some people, adding this exercise to their routine would be beneficial. However, I recommend performing the BackSmart Daily Dozen stretches before doing yoga, to help prepare the body for those long holding positions, and doing the shower stretches afterward to relieve muscle soreness. Additionally, once you have developed back or neck pain, I think you have to be careful when practicing yoga because many positions put a large amount of torque on your spine, which could lead to further complications in the small joints in your spine.

As with all other activities, there are good yoga instructors and bad ones. If you think you'd like to take a yoga class, check around and ask if you can watch a week's worth of sessions before joining. See if the instructor gives modified positions for students who cannot perform the movements due to their lack of flexibility. If the instructor is rigid in his or her methods and requires everyone to execute the exercises as described, I recommend you go elsewhere.

USING THE BACKSMART METHOD SUCCESSFULLY

Finally let's review some maintenance tips for the successful new you using the BackSmart Method. Keep in mind that most injuries from exercise are strains, the result of overstressing or overstretching muscles and/or tendons. Proper warm-up, stretching beforehand, and proper lifting technique help to prevent strain. Once a strain occurs, you need to rest the area. Other aids to healing may include the use of ice to keep down swelling, elevation to promote venous return of blood, and compression. Later in the healing process, heat can be used, including ultrasound to smooth out the tendon and muscle fibers.

In cases of light or moderate strain, it is often unnecessary to pinpoint exactly where in a complex structure the strain has occurred. You can feel which general area is involved, and you can tell which movements aggravate the damage so that you can avoid working that area. Strain can occur in areas that you are not actually working but simply contracting for leverage. Most joint injuries that exercisers incur are a result of years of wear and tear on the body. These problems build up slowly.

Younger people may train hard and not notice any problems, but in later years they can pay the price of this physical abuse. Younger exercisers have greater recuperative powers and can bounce back from injuries faster than older exercisers. As you grow older and continue to train, there are things you can't get away with—training methods that would not have resulted in injury in your youth but that will once you are older and your body has suffered from years of strain. This may involve a change in training style.

If you travel a lot and want to be able to keep up with workouts while you're on the road, try to do more walking and incorporate the BackSmart Daily Dozen into your schedule if it's a short trip. Wall stretches with an ab routine can be done in a hotel room. If you're on a longer trip, remember that most hotels today have their own exercise facilities. Or you can ask someone at the front desk where the nearest gym is located.

When doing cardio in workouts, do not get caught up in the amount of time you are putting in, as long as you do it. Studies have shown that doing aerobic workouts on an empty stomach in the morning has the greatest potential for fat loss. On the other hand, if you have only the evenings to exercise, you will burn the calories that you consumed during the day.

While you want to be careful, don't be afraid to change your routine frequently and keep your body challenged to avoid getting into a fitness rut. Also do not let your fears get in your way of trying a new activity. Don't give up because you are unable to perform a certain amount of repetitions. Anxiety is normal when you're starting something new. Be persistent and try new movements. Break them down into smaller ranges of motion to get the feel for each before trying the whole routine.

Remember, there is no particular age at which to start the program, and if you have kids, it would be a good idea to start them on it now and possibly ward off future injuries as they learn the proper way to exercise and stretch out their bodies. This will also reinforce the healthy habit of exercise. So, have fun and enjoy your workout!

CONCLUSION

I hope you have enjoyed what the BackSmart exercises have to offer you for a new healthy outlook on life. At the beginning of this book, I assured you satisfaction with your results if you invested the time and effort into following my recommendations. I hope you have. Constantly strive to improve the way you feel as your body moves through the exercises, and focus on the big picture: a pain-free, strong, flexible, athletic body and a sound mind. For further information regarding The BackSmart Fitness Plan search the Internet, key words BackSmart or Dr. Adam Weiss.

INDEX